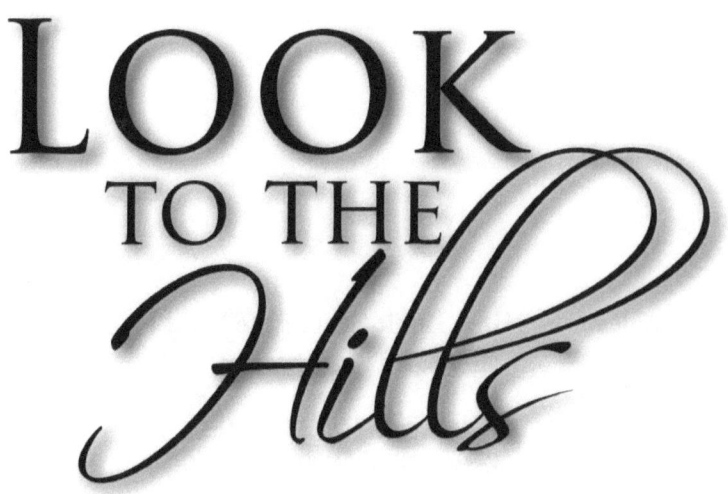

BOOK ONE OF THE WEST HOPE TRILOGY

MARY JEAN BONAR

Look to the Hills: Book One of the West Hope Trilogy
Copyright © 2024 by Mary Jean Bonar

ISBN: 978-1639458738 (sc)
ISBN: 978-1639458745 (e)

Library of Congress Control Number: 2012916417

All rights reserved. No part of this publication may be reproduced, distributed, or transmitted in any form or by any means, including photocopying, recording, or other electronic or mechanical methods, without the prior written permission of the publisher and/or the author, except in the case of brief quotations embodied in critical reviews and other noncommercial uses permitted by copyright law.

The views expressed in this book are solely those of the author and do not necessarily reflect the views of the publisher, and the publisher hereby disclaims any responsibility for them.

Writers' Branding
(877) 608-6550
www.writersbranding.com
media@writersbranding.com

To God be the Glory!

I lift up my eyes to the hills.
From where does my help come?
My help comes from the Lord
who made heaven and earth
Psalm 121:1-2 ESV

Mary Jean Bonar's first novel *Overflowing with Hope* received many endorsements including:

"I am convinced that Mary Jean Bonar was inspired when she wrote Overflowing with Hope *and I believe the reader will feel the inspiration while reading this delightful account of one woman's spiritual experiences, her personal relationships, and the lovely community in which she resides. If connecting with characters in the story is a test of a good novel, this book passes the test beautifully."*

> J.W. George Wallace, Editor/Publisher,
> The Brooke County Review

". . . What a beautiful Story. I can't stop thinking about the beautiful women in the story and what a difference one person can make when she is in tune with God . . ."

> Nancy L. Griffin, Board of Directors
> of Public Library in Yale, OK

"Overflowing with Hope" stands in the face of all the negativity surrounding us, and claims that we can rise above the forces. This story helps me realize that ordinary people can become quite extraordinary when they gain God's hope. People are enabled to face the small and large crises of everyday living with strength and courage that they obtained when viewing life through God's eyes. God's vision brings God's hope, an overflowing hope that our world so desperately needs.

> Dr. Jack Emerick (The author's pastor)

"Our book club just finished reading your book Overflowing with Hope *and then we shared it with other groups in the church. One impact that the book has made on our congregation is how we view elderly people in our church and in society in general."*

Janet Kiaski, United Methodist Church of Richmond, Ohio

", , , Overflowing with Hope was very inspirational for me. I loved the way you interjected scripture into the story line. Being newly retired I am attending a Women of Faith study group with women of the church, many of whom are much older than I am. Thanks for writing a book I can learn from and recommend to my friends."

Carole Waugh, Retired Nurse, Mt. Vernon, Ohio

Contents

Prologue	A Day the Lord Has Made	1
Chapter 1	Life in the Fast Lane	5
Chapter 2	Working the Night Shift	17
Chapter 3	Wedding I	23
Chapter 4	Wedding II	25
Chapter 5	The Family Portrait	34
Chapter 6	The Western Front	44
Chapter 7	Benefits?	46
Chapter 8	Easter Preparations	49
Chapter 9	He Is Risen!	54
Chapter 10	Picture This!	63
Chapter 11	Out of Focus	67
Chapter 12	Blowing in the Wind	70
Chapter 13	Is Anybody Listening?	76
Chapter 14	The Ladies of West Hope	79
Chapter 15	A "Stirring"	87
Chapter 16	The Winds of Change	90
Chapter 17	Calling the Realtor	98
Chapter 18	Moving On?	106

Chapter 19	*Coming Home*	*111*
Chapter 20	*Julia Remembers*	*115*
Chapter 21	*Puddles and Obstacles*	*119*
Chapter 22	*Rachael Ventures Out*	*122*
Chapter 23	*A Praying People*	*129*
Chapter 24	*Morning Has Broken*	*133*
Chapter 25	*Decisions, Decisions*	*139*
Chapter 26	*Two by Two*	*145*
Chapter 27	*Apple-Blossom Time*	*148*
Chapter 28	*From Scene to Shining Scene*	*152*
Chapter 29	*Opening Doors*	*157*
Chapter 30	*"Click"*	*172*
Chapter 31	*They Come and They Go*	*182*
Chapter 32	*A "Getaway"*	*188*
Chapter 33	*She's Floored*	*193*
Chapter 34	*Holding On*	*201*

Q and A for the Author 208

About the Author 210

Characters of note in *Look to the Hills* 211

Prologue

A Day the Lord Has Made

Janine was eager to enter into the freshness of a new day as she walked outside after the rain. She looked up and greeted the Lord and slowly drew in a deep breath. *Could the sky be bluer? Mmm . . . and that sweet fragrance. What is it?*

She began to look around. Her red and white petunias were growing nicely where she had planted them as the outer rim of a circular floral garden. It would be at least a month before they would completely fill in the spaces, but they were standing strong, and the reds were vibrant with the color. The grass throughout the yard was Scotland green. Everything appeared fresh and alive in the clearness of the spring morning . . . But what *is* that lovely fragrance?

Something caught her eye. There at the side of the driveway were the peonies she had planted last summer, and one was finally in full bloom! The flower was a soft pink, just as she had remembered at her home as a child. Her parents had many such bushes—some white, some deep pink—but this soft pink had been her mother's favorite and hers as well.

She had been waiting for the bloom, and there it was, stretching toward her as though to say, "I'm here because you wanted me to be. I'm here for your pleasure. Come and enjoy." It was beautiful. *How many petals does a peony have?* She wondered. *There must be hundreds, each embracing the others just as God had planned for them to do.*

Her heart beat faster, and she gently walked toward the flower as though she dared not disturb it, as though it was sacred. And truly it was, because it was a gift from God Himself. Yes, she had planted it, but it was His creation, and the joy of her thankfulness was as exquisite as the morning and the pink peony beckoning to her.

Slowly, slowly she walked, and unmistakably the fragrance intensified. She drew near, not yet bending for the fullness of the scent, savoring every second. She bent her knees, leaned forward, and there it was, just as she had known it would be—the sweetest fragrance of her youth. The memory was vivid as she closed her eyes and drank in the aroma. She was back in time, a precious time, when her mother and father would bend with her to smell the peonies. She felt their presence, and it was bliss. She fell to her knees, tears of joy on her cheeks, and with heartfelt gratitude praised God—not only for this day of days but also because she knew that her memories, her life today and all she would ever be, were because of His love and care for her.

"Father in Heaven, you have given me so much today that I cannot take it all in." She forced herself to continue her walk, but she would not forget to settle down later and completely observe the blessed day, enjoy it, and be thankful.

It was a beautiful morning indeed, after the rain, on a Tuesday in early June as she reluctantly left the peony and began her morning walk, reflecting upon her days just a year or so ago of structured busyness, of self-demanding accomplishments and the swirl of events that brought her to these shining days of appreciation and wonder.

A YEAR OR SO AGO

1

Life in the Fast Lane

Janine's week had been busy from minute to minute as life continued to gather speed. Her position at Center Church as director of music had expanded to include monitoring three choirs, directing occasionally, and serving as principal organist. Her head was always full of planning, and rehearsals were especially intense during the holy seasons for the church year.

It might have been easier if she didn't have "flexible" hours. A nine-to-five job was beginning to be a fantasy in her mind. Nevertheless, she loved her work at the church, and now that her three children were gone from the nest, her schedule was a little less complicated, at least.

But why did she say yes to the presidency of the Women's Association? It was much more demanding of her than she had anticipated; nevertheless, she knew she could do it, and no one else was going to. Her deepest frustration came nearly every evening when bedtime rolled around and she had no time or clarity of mind to turn her attention to her writing. The book was unwritten. Her research files were incomplete. She was constantly setting her dream aside.

Oh well. Maybe next year, she thought as she brushed away the fleeting moment. Next year . . . Hadn't she said that many times before?

She had spent several hours at the church going through the files of music to decide upon worship music for the rapidly approaching holy seasons of Lent and Easter. She would spend more time tomorrow studying through the new music she had ordered.

Charlotte, the new choir director, preferred that Janine continue to choose the music for the adult choir while she was becoming more familiar with the capabilities of the singers. Janine realized and understood the comfort of singing familiar anthems, but she was not one to take the effortless path. She liked to challenge the choirs and herself to always be learning, progressing, and giving their best. Charlotte was in complete agreement.

She stepped into the church office and spoke with Connie, a secretary with exceptional abilities. She was indispensable to a smooth-running church and could be counted upon for accuracy and promptness. Janine appreciated those qualities and especially enjoyed Connie and her loving interest in the entire congregation.

"Good morning, Connie," she said. "How are you, and how are things at home?"

"Well, good morning to you. I'm great and things have calmed down at home, somewhat. The Lord has been good to us. Richard is recovering well from the surgery and feeling stronger every day, and he is now able to take care of his personal needs for the most part."

"That's terrific. I know that he does not like to depend upon someone else. That would be hard for me too, and probably would be for you as well. We'll keep praying for him. He'll be back to work good as new before we know it."

"He has a doctor's appointment next week. He's determined to convince the doctor that he's ready to return, but I'm not so sure . . . We'll see," Connie said.

"Is Pastor Jim in?"

"He was here a few minutes ago, but when he called Mabel Morrison's family this morning, he found that she was not doing very well. You know how he is. He was out of here in a flash."

"He's a good man and a wonderful pastor," Janine said. "I'll check in with him in the morning. Nothing important. I need to get moving, anyway. See you tomorrow!"

"Okay. Be careful out there. Looks like it might snow. I think it's supposed to today."

"That's what I heard. I hope it holds off. I have errands to run, groceries to buy, and two piano students coming later this afternoon. I'd really better get moving. Take care. Bye."

As she got into her car, she picked up the note on the seat. *Hmm, let's see. Should I stop over at the coffee shop and get a sandwich or just keep going? I'd better keep going and go to the drive-through for coffee. No time for food right now, and it looks like those clouds are forming into something ominous.*

I'll go to the post office first, grab a coffee, and then take the overpass around to Gloria's Gift Shop to pick up the vase I ordered for the wedding. I'll have it gift-wrapped. How long will that take? Gloria can be so slow sometimes, but she does a beautiful job. Okay, I'll have her do it. It might actually save time in the long run; then I'll go to the supermarket on that side of town. That'll work!

The coffee was too hot, so she set it in the cupholder and proceeded to the highway around the city. "What's this? Oh, not again!" Traffic was almost at a standstill, and there was no turning back from the entrance ramp with cars in front and behind. This was getting to be almost commonplace as scores of business travelers and convoys of trucks were on the roads.

She crept along, drank all the coffee, and finally was on her way—if one could construe moving at 25 mph as "on the way." What was the holdup this time? "Uh-oh!" Flashing lights were all over the road ahead. Her heart skipped as she worried that someone was hurt. An eighteen-wheeler was overturned with traffic limited to one lane, and very slowly at that. She turned on the radio and flipped from station to station to find some news concerning the accident. All she found was a nationally broadcast talk show. She'd have to wait for the news on the hour. In the meantime, she was passing the accident. Nothing else was involved, but the truck was on its side. It looked like the driver was standing there, unhurt. Thankfully.

She passed the congestion and moved on, this time at a more normal speed, and arrived at the exit and to Gloria's much, much later than she had planned.

"Hi, Gloria. My goodness, the traffic today was so slow. Once again, an eighteen-wheeler tried to make that turn at Exit 10 too fast. He turned over. Why, oh why can't they follow the caution signs? I don't think he was hurt. At least, I hope not. Anyway, I'm here to pick up the vase."

"Oh, sweetie, you're just going to love it. It's beautiful, and the bride will be thrilled. I'll go get it for you."

Gloria could have stood in for Dolly Parton with her blond hair, fantastic smile, and eagerness to please. When anyone walked into her shop, she found an immediate friend in Gloria. *"The world needs more people like her,"* Janine thought.

Her shop was exquisite. Janine always tried to purchase her special gifts here. She looked around while Gloria was in the back. As always, new items were on the shelves and tables to catch her eye and her attention. Gloria had an eye for beautiful glass, unusual carvings, imported paper products, linens, and more. Gloria returned quickly with the vase, which was a good thing because she felt tempted to look at the beautiful table setting on the other side of the room, and who knew where that would lead?

"This is perfect!" she said when Gloria took the vase out of the box. Imported from Italy, it was shaped into an alluring form and painted with deeply colorful flowers. Anyone would be pleased to have it. Janine was delighted that she had ordered it and asked Gloria to wrap it for her. They decided upon the wrapping, and surprisingly, Gloria moved right along.

"How is your handsome husband and Kathy and her family?" Gloria asked.

"John's great. Busy as usual, but aren't we all? Kathy and her husband love their log home in the beautiful hills. I'm beginning to understand why she moved from the city. The only noise is the song of birds or, in the distance, the bawling of a cow. It's quite a different life for them. The girls have adjusted very well, so the move proved to be a good one. I thought we wouldn't see them much, but John and I love going to their home. It's almost like a retreat in a quiet part of the world, so we do get out often."

"Must be nice," Gloria said. "Well, here you are. How's that?"

"Gloria, you are so talented. Beautifully done! Thank you so much. And thank you for your suggestion about the vase." She paid her, said her good-bye, and was out of the door in decent time after all. She was all smiles and very satisfied that the vase was just right.

Now, I have barely enough time to shop for the groceries, get home, put them away, put the casserole in the oven, freshen up, teach, and have dinner ready on time. I can do it. *I just have to stay focused.*

ᵞᵞᵞ

She was taking the casserole from the oven when John drove up from work. Perfect timing! Janine liked everything nice and tidy, on time, and done right! She was a bride of the fifties and, consequently, a *Leave It to Beaver* kind of mom and housewife. And even though Betty Freidan's book and the ultimate change in society led most women away from homemaking aspiration, she still did her best to adhere to the values and standards of a woman's role in the home. It was more difficult now with her position at the church, her volunteer work in the community, and teaching; but she was not going to hire help to do her *real* job—that of maintaining an orderly home. Her daughter Kathy reminded her constantly that she was over-the-top in seeing that everything was in its place, the furniture was polished, the windows shining, and that dishes matched the occasion, but she turned a deaf ear to all that. She knew what was right. She could do it, and so she would!

Today she was using her Pfaltzgraff Orleans pattern that had a casserole to match. The dishes were blue on white with a tiny orange flower scattered along the edging. She used a white tablecloth, napkins of deep blue, and a centerpiece of fresh lilies in orange that she had picked up at the supermarket. The flowers would bring a little sunshine into the room on this very gloomy wintry day.

Perfect!

I'll just put these utensils in the dishwasher and straighten up and all will be on time when John comes in. Mmm . . . The casserole looks great, and John will enjoy the Mandarin orange salad and fresh rolls from the market bakery.

There he is. I'll undo the apron and put it in the drawer. She greeted him at the door and was happy to see him.

They were blessed with a good marriage and were both totally satisfied and secure in their love and companionship for one another. This was one of the best moments of every day. She thanked God for giving her such a good man to share her life with.

"Hi, honey," she said as he came through the door. "Hi, babe," he responded. "How was your day?"

"Good. Dinner's ready. I know you have a board meeting at the church tonight, so I thought you'd want to eat early."

"Oh, that's right! Janine, can you hold up on dinner for a while? I want to talk with you about something. How about getting us each a cup of coffee and come and sit down?"

"John, what is it?" He was clearly upset, and she was getting nervous. "Is it one of the children?"

"No, no, nothing like that." "Did someone die?"

"No. Honey, go ahead and turn down the stove or whatever. Okay?"

"Okay." She moved on into the kitchen. Everything—absolutely everything she could think of—was going through her mind. It had to be something pretty traumatic. He was ashen and obviously shaken. She hurried and covered the casserole with foil, put it in a very low oven, rewrapped the rolls, and put the salads in the refrigerator. She poured two cups of coffee and took them to the living room where he was sitting in his favorite chair.

"Here you are," she said and sat down in her favorite place on the sofa. "Now."

"Okay. You remember last week when there were rumbles about a major layoff in the company?"

She nodded.

"Well, we figured wrong when we guessed it would be the very youngest employed. They have decided to begin the layoffs at the upper level. They believe that they can save more money that way because the senior workers have the highest wages—which, of course, they've earned over the years."

She decided to say nothing. She knew what was coming and thought it best to let him tell it as he thought he should.

"Late this afternoon, Jack called me into his office. It didn't take long for me to figure out what was happening. He said he was sorry, of course, but he had to do what the company told him to do. I am finished there. Gone . . . *kaput*! I cleaned out my desk, and that's it. I mean, no warnings, and probably no benefits. Well, that's not exactly the way they said it. They said there would be a benefit meeting for all discharged employees to *explain* the remaining benefits. So maybe we'll have some kind of income and insurance, I don't know."

"John, how many others did they let go?"

"Looks like a lot. Not many were talking, but I saw others carrying out boxes of their personal items just as I was doing. They gave us boxes. Everything is in the box: all that I have meant to the company for thirty-three years. One box and no good-bye."

ϒϒϒ

They did a lot of talking about possibilities while they were having dinner, although neither of them managed to eat more than a few bites of food. Janine knew it was going to be a difficult transition for John and for her, but she believed that in time things would be all right. John was well educated, a very good accountant, and had been in a supervisory position for quite a few years. But it must have been a terribly degrading blow to him to be cast aside for younger workers who didn't have enough knowledge of the company to care about its future.

Before they knew it, time ran out, and John had to leave for the board meeting. She turned on the porch light and saw that the snow was beginning to fall, and naturally, she was worried about him going out. He kissed her and assured her he would be fine with four-wheel drive and said the snow probably wouldn't amount to much.

She watched his taillights disappear in the snow, kept the porch light on for his return, and busied herself cleaning up. She felt rather shaky with all the events of the day and couldn't calm herself down. She thought about John. He was always there for her, encouraging her through everything. *What would I do without him?* Why did she think such thoughts? She wasn't losing John. Obviously, life would certainly be different now, but they would face whatever came to them together.

She began to feel sad and then actually angry with the company for their inconsiderate discharging of loyal employees. She asked herself the eternal question asked by generations before. *What's wrong with the world these days?* Whatever happened to trust and reliability in the workplace? How can those people be comfortable with carelessly bruising the lives of those who have been so faithful?

Anger took over. She wanted to fight back but knew that would do no good. She now felt frustration along with the anger, and the snow continued to fall! Nothing felt right. She wanted to pray, and she knew that she needed the comfort and strength she would feel with the Lord close to her, but she chose to go on worrying instead.

Look at that snow coming down. She stood in the window watching for John to return.

He should have been home by now. Maybe I should call the church and see if he is still there. No, that might disturb the meeting. I'll give it a little more time.

She walked over to the organ. She had planned to review the wedding music this evening, so maybe if she concentrated on that, it would ease her mind somewhat. A former piano student was getting married. It would be such a pleasure to play for her wedding as she wished her blessings and happiness with her marriage. The rehearsal would be tomorrow. She had performed this wedding music many times and shouldn't have any problems with any of it. Cindy was not having a soloist, which always made it easier for the organist. So she lined up the music in order and started with the first, hoping that this exercise would settle her down somewhat.

She began with J. S. Bach's "Arioso" and was soon in another world. Music always did that for her. As she enjoyed the twenty-minute prelude and was ready for the processional, she looked over at the clock and her heart skipped.

"John is still not home! I'm going to call the church, or the police, or something," she said aloud.

As she reached for the telephone, she saw automobile lights turning into the driveway and hoped and prayed with all her might that it was John and not the police.

She ran to the door just as John was opening up the garage. "Oh, thank you, Lord. Thank you," she said as she waited in the open doorway, not noticing the snow swirling in her face at all.

When John came over to her, she embraced him intensely with relief.

"John, I was worried about you. Is everything all right?"

"I'm sorry, honey. I should have called you. The meeting went well and everyone was eager to get on home, so we broke up rather quickly. I felt the need to talk with Pastor Jim, and I'm so glad I did. He's really a wonderful person to share with. He prayed with me and helped me to know that everything is not lost. He pointed clearly to scripture that tells us that God is in control of our lives and that we need not be concerned with what tomorrow brings. You know what? Whatever tomorrow brings, God will be there!"

"Well, that is a very comforting thought. 'God will be there.'"

"I know. That's one thing we can count on, Janine. So what else do we need? We have so much to be thankful for. I suppose we could count for days the many blessings we do have, so we need to focus upon those—put our lives in God's able hands and trust in Him. How easy is that?" he asked, smiling from ear to ear.

Janine smiled back, overflowing with her gratitude once again for John and the stability he had always brought her. "Everything's going to be fine," she said and wished that she could trust as wholeheartedly as John did.

2

Working the Night Shift

A friend had told Janine once that she was a "problem solver," and she believed that was correct. Janine thought she could fix anything that needed it if it was within her realm of operation, so turning everything over to God wasn't so easy for her. John seemed to be sleeping like a baby. Good for him! Well, if he and God needed any help, she'd try to be ready, but she would not interfere unless John asked her for an opinion.

She always had an opinion, that's for sure. That was definitely not a problem with her. She had one, and she would be glad to share it with almost anybody.

She slept fitfully. She had too many thoughts racing through her head. They needed to call the children and tell them about the change that had occurred today, and of course, she knew they would be concerned. She and John would do everything they could to assure them that they need not worry. She thought of Kathy in her amiable home with a beautiful family and how happy and at peace she had been lately. She thought of their younger daughter Deborah, living in a lovely development just outside of Pittsburgh—she a teacher and her husband a medical doctor, their lives enwrapped in a social whirl. She began to drift off as she thought of Harry and his family of boys in Oklahoma. Harry's sons were rootin', tootin' little guys enjoying the outdoors and the casual living of the South.

What time is it? Oh my gosh! It's two o'clock. I'm never going to get through the day tomorrow!

"Lord, help me to calm down. My head is buzzing with too many things tonight."

Would He help her? She believed He would if only she could let go of her own sense of doing it all. The prayer was not answered.

ϒϒϒ

She awakened to a sense that something was changed, but she was not sure just what it was. She immediately noticed that John was not beside her, and looking at the clock, she knew why. It was 8:32 a.m. She never slept beyond six o'clock! But then, she couldn't get to sleep last night, so no wonder she slept late.

She hurried out of bed, freshened up, and when she walked into the kitchen, she faced the "something that was different." There stood John, grinning from ear to ear, in his "Dad Cooks Best" apron stirring a delicious-looking omelet.

"Well, this is nice," she said. "Why didn't you wake me?" "You were sleeping and snoring. I figured you needed more rest, and since I was up with no plans for the day, I decided to fix us a nice breakfast, take it easy, and get acquainted." He laughed.

"You silly goose. That's really sweet, but I have so much to do today. I'd better just get my shower, grab a bite on the run, and get going. I've already missed my morning walk."

She saw his disappointment. She really should stay, but her schedule was packed for the day, and she hadn't expected to find herself with a husband home and wanting to spend time with her. She was torn. What to do?

She looked outside and saw that the snowfall from the night before was practically melted, so the roads should be no problem. She had an appointment at ten o'clock with some of the women from the church who were planning an association event. She could call them and push it to eleven, skip lunch, and get on with the music plan.

"John, you're right. We really should get acquainted after sleeping together last night . . . so let me make a quick phone call. Do you need any help here?"

"Nope." He smiled, and she knew she had made the right decision. "Everything's taken care of. I'll pour the juice and the coffee and set things out while you do the telephoning. Don't be long. Okay?"

"Okay."

She looked up the number and made one call. It would be fine. She felt that she should go fix herself up for this man who had suddenly made himself at home in her kitchen, so she fussed a tiny little bit with her hair, put on some light makeup and a pretty robe, and was back in the kitchen in a flash.

John was whistling, and when she came into the kitchen, he pulled out a chair for her and they had the nicest breakfast.

How special it was, and when had they ever had this kind of time without being on a vacation or something? She tried not to look at the clock, but she just couldn't resist. She was still good on time, and she knew it meant a lot to John that they sit and talk awhile this morning, so she tried to concentrate on that.

"Looks like the snow is going to melt away," John said. "I didn't know if I'd be shoveling this morning or not. It was still coming down when I went to sleep last night."

"Honey, I was thinking. Do you think we should call the kids, or wait until the weekend?" Janine asked.

"Well, there's really no hurry. We probably should try to get ourselves oriented a little before rushing to the phone. Here's what I think. How about if we call Deborah and Bob and Kathy and Greg and see if we can meet with all of them on Sunday afternoon? Maybe at Kathy's. We don't have to say anything about why. I could call Kathy today and see if it's okay with them and ask her if she'd like to invite Deb and Bob. How's that sound?"

"Fine with me. It would be nice to get together anyway, and all we really have to say is that you were laid off and we aren't sure what we'll want to do about it . . . but not to worry. We are not going to be in any kind of trouble or anything like that . . . right?"

"Right. I also will want to go to the benefits meeting before jumping to conclusions about anything at all. We'll do okay, Jan. You know I've been fairly faithful to put aside something for our latter years, so maybe they've popped up a little sooner than we expected."

"I know I've grumbled about you doing that sometimes, John. I'm sorry. You were right all along. And I still have the work at the church, and that little bit will help out too. We will want to sit down and look at the entire picture. You are so good at balancing budgets. I know you'll set us on the right track." John smiled and seemed very confident. She hoped he wasn't trying to cover his anxieties, but she truly believed he was not.

They agreed on John calling Kathy. He said he had some things he could do during the day with his car that would keep him busy and dirty, which he loved.

She started to pick up the breakfast dishes.

"Hey! I can do that," he said. "You go ahead and get ready for your meeting."

"Well, that's nice." She gave him a hug and headed for the shower. She would be a very busy gal all day, and she realized that her life might change a lot. Would John want to begin his daily routines with breakfast together and morning conversation with her? That sounded so good, but it absolutely would not work on a daily basis. She liked to drink some coffee, eat a banana, and go for a walk early. The walk was necessary for her physical and spiritual health, and she needed both to get her day off on the right foot. Then she could get a shower while thinking over her upcoming day, get dressed, gather up her necessary items, and move along.

Things will be different now. They'd have to work it out together. I hope he finds something to do to occupy himself. He's too young to just live a retiree's life and have nothing substantial to do. That could really complicate things with her life, which was controlled by obligations every minute of the day, but she also realized that John wouldn't be content just sitting around. He would find other interests. There's no point in thinking this way.

Since she couldn't know what the future would hold, she decided to put that aside and get on with the business at hand.

3
Wedding I

Saturday turned into quite an adventure with more interruptions than usual. Nothing important, really, but nothing ran smoothly. Janine had to hurry to get to the wedding. She did not like to do that. She always wanted to be at a wedding at least forty minutes before the ceremony so that she could collect herself and her music and be ready to enjoy playing a twenty-minute prelude segment.

She and John went flying down the road. John parked the car, and Janine went on in without him. And of course, she ran into someone she hadn't seen in a long time who wanted to talk, talk, talk. She excused herself graciously as soon as she could as John came through the door. She gave him a well-understood look of frustration with the situation and went directly to the organ.

The church was filling up quickly, and she should have been playing. *Calm down, girl!* she told herself. You still have the twenty minutes you planned on using for the prelude. Just get on with it!

She turned on the organ, pushed all the right buttons, and began with the Bach "Arioso" as she had planned. This was one of her all-time favorites, and it sounded so beautiful in the large sanctuary. She knew everything was going to be all right as the music soothed her soul; she was beginning to enjoy herself. The rehearsal had gone like clockwork last night, and she knew what to expect from the minister and the wedding party. It would be fine, and Cindy, the bride, would appreciate her gift to her today.

The couple was being announced as "Mr. and Mrs." and everyone applauded. She peeked around the music and watched the kiss that really was a kiss and then began Jean-Joseph Mouret's "Rondeau" for the recessional. How exciting. She had one of the best jobs in the world! She loved the music. She loved the organ, and it was such a blessing to be able to assist the sacred ceremony in this beautiful way.

She and John went to the reception. They didn't know many of the guests, and that meant that they could be together and not get lost in a crowd of conversations. They danced most of the evening and felt so secure in their love, wishing the bride and groom the same loving relationship with one another. After a nice slow dance, they said good night to the bride and groom and Cindy's family and took their leave.

Weddings. They definitely have a way of exposing what's right with relationships and bringing longtime couples to a fresh awareness of the joy of marriage and commitment to one another. Janine and John were thankful for their marriage, and once again, they felt comfort in the assurance of their love.

4

Wedding II

That Sunday afternoon, as they were driving to Kathy's, John said, "Greg seemed genuinely excited that we could come today. What was it he said he wanted to prepare for us to eat?"

"Wait a minute. You wrote it down, didn't you? It was a new recipe with turkey, wasn't it?"

"Oh yes. It was sesame-crusted turkey mignons. I remember. I couldn't spell 'mignons.' It will be served with some kind of creamy wine sauce. And there would be éclairs. I forget the rest."

"He's such a good cook. Anything he does is just yummy, but I could have taken something for the meal, or we could have had soup and sandwich. But that's Greg. Gone are the days when 'Mama' does the cooking in this family."

"Well, honey, you are still a very good cook, and you do a lot of it in our house, so enjoy it when you have the opportunity to sit down to a meal without being in the kitchen all day."

"Thanks. I will, believe me."

The drive over was very pleasant as the roads were completely clear, and the grasses on the country hills were still splashed with the freshness of snow. Everything was quiet and peaceful, and they welcomed it all.

John knew that Janine always enjoyed driving past the old row houses in West Hope, and so he took the longer way that went directly through the borough.

For some strange reason that she couldn't understand, something seemed to be calling her there. She felt a very close connection with the community even though she had never met anyone who lived there. And she'd had dreams of West Hope—of sitting on someone's porch, walking through the backyards, and talking with the people. It was just the strangest thing.

As they rounded the bend past the apple orchard entering the eastern end of the town, Janine said, "Someday I'd like to park here and walk past all of the houses. Maybe I could find someone to talk with, and then perhaps I can discover what is in this town that draws me to it. There's not much here really except that quaint little grocery store, a beauty shop, and a post office.

"Oh, look! The church on the knoll there seems to have had a celebration today. Look at the parking lot. It's full to the limit . . . Yes! See the sign? *Congratulations Francine and Lawrence.*"

It was a wedding.

"They must have gotten married right after church and had a reception there," John said.

"Could be," said Janine as they continued on past the post office and the row houses. They were soon out of town, turning onto McDade Road and on through the countryside for a few miles through a rural settlement of a few scattered houses. They made a right turn onto Bear Track Lane.

The snow still lingered there in the wooded areas where tire tracks provided easy access on toward Kathy's.

Meanwhile, back at the church, the members and guests were joyfully celebrating a wedding. Iola, Beatrice, Virginia, Adele, and others were busy in the kitchen finishing up the dishes.

"Once again, we have too many leftovers," Adele said. "Our church has the world's best cooks. Iola, would you look in the corner cupboard and see if the carryout boxes are there?" Virginia asked.

Iola found them, and they began to package up beans, beets, potatoes, salads, ham, and fried chicken for the city mission, which Pastor Dan had volunteered to deliver.

The "hit" of the meal was the cake donated and decorated by Beatrice Roberts. It was in three tiers with a bride and groom holding hands on the top.

Around the top tier were the words "Love is Patient." Around the second tier, "Love is Kind." And around the bottom, "Love is God's Gift." It was very beautifully done, and everyone said it was the most perfect cake for this wedding there could ever be.

It was the first marriage for Francine Cook and Lawrence Simmons, and they had waited a long time to find one another.

Everyone was so happy they were married. Fran had always trusted that God would send her husband to her, even though God's clock and hers were not always ticking along together.

℣℣℣

Larry had come to the church at the invitation of Paula Kirkland, a relative of the Cooks. Fran was the organist at the church, and one morning, Kevin Kirkland was standing behind her after the postlude; and when she finished, he said, "Francine, I'd like you to meet Lawrence Simmons."

She had noticed Lawrence sitting with Kevin and Paula for a few weeks and wondered who he was. He was quite good-looking, seemed about her age, and was taller than most of the congregation.

"Your music is very nice," Lawrence said.

"Thank you," she replied, suddenly not knowing what else to say.

Kevin said, "Lawrence is from Emerson Mills and has just retired from Gerald Publishing. I told him that you are a schoolteacher, so you both obviously have an interest in books."

Well. That's certainly reaching long and hard for a mutual interest.

"I see," she said, frustrated with her inability to find words to say. This had never been a problem for her.

She began assembling her music and closing up the organ as Lawrence said, "Well, see you next week."

"Yes. Nice to meet you," she said.

ᲥᲥᲥ

The next day, Monday, Paula called.

"Hi, cuz," she said. "How's Aunt Alice today?" "She's very well, thank you."

No one would ever guess that Alice Cook is eighty-seven years old. She still maintains her own home and has a very sharp mind and memory. She is well known around the church to have the answer to any Bible trivia question.

"That's wonderful," Paula said. "Kevin and I were wondering if you would like to come to dinner on Friday evening—you and Aunt Alice. Lawrence Simmons is coming, and we'd like for him to become better acquainted with some of our church members. He seems interested in the church, and we want to encourage him to continue."

"Well, that sounds nice. I'll ask Mother, but I think you can count on us. What can I bring?"

"Nothing . . . nothing. It will be simple. No problem. Come around six o'clock if you can."

"Well, thank you very much. See you at six."

Francine didn't know it then, but Paula was working as a matchmaker for the Master, for if ever a match were made in Heaven, this would be it!

Francine and Alice drove over the rolling hills on that lovely summer evening with expectations of a pleasant evening. It was that, all right, and much, much more.

Laura and Edward Davidson were there. They owned the adjoining farm, and both families raised cattle. Anne and Owen Kendrick were there also. The men were sitting on the porch talking about the herds, and they stood when Francine and Alice arrived.

"Good evening, ladies, and welcome! Sit down a spell if you'd like to. It's a perfect evening for rockin' and talkin'," Kevin said.

"Good evening, Ms. Alice and Francine," Edward said. "It's nice to see ya! The ladies are inside fixin' up something that smells mighty good."

"Ladies," said Owen, tipping his hat.

"Good evening, gentlemen," the ladies responded.

"I think I'll go on inside and see what they're up to," said Alice.

"I think I will too." Fran smiled, and said, "Enjoy your rockin' and talkin'."

"That we will," said Edward. "That we will," he repeated as he and the other two gentlemen sat down.

The ladies had everything in good order, so they sat down in the parlor and talked about such things as women are likely to find interesting.

Anne asked Paula how her latest quilt was coming along. Anne, a meticulous quilter, had been Paula's mentor on quilting, and they sometimes quilted together.

"I finally finished it! Would you like to see it?"

They all were quick to respond that they would and soon were climbing up the beautiful curved staircase to the front bedroom. There on the bed was one of the most beautiful quilts any of them had ever seen! It was a pattern from the nineteenth century, with squares no larger than an inch. There were hundreds of them, and the colors were of faded blues, rose, and white in a fascinating pattern. It was delicate and exquisitely finished and must have taken many hours to complete.

Beatrice said, "Paula, you have outdone yourself! You must enter this into the Applewood Fair this year!"

"Not only that fair, but any and all that you can. It is magnificent," said Anne as she fingered the stitches and smoothed it over. What a compliment from one of the best!

They all agreed, and Paula said she didn't know, but she'd give it some consideration.

"Well, you'd better! I'm tellin' you," Bea said.

Alice thought that the ladies in that small gathering were all of special talents. Paula's fabulous piecing, matching, and sewing; Francine's gift of music; Bea's cake decorating; Anne, who could stitch up just about anything; and Laura's baking and glorious gladiolus that won many a blue ribbon.

They heard a car door and turned immediately to thoughts of the dinner and welcoming the special guest of the evening. "Come with me and greet Larry, and then we'll put dinner on the table," Paula said.

Larry shyly walked up the stone sidewalk lined with multicolored impatiens. The men on the porch stood. *My goodness*, he thought as he saw a group of women bursting from the front screen door.

Paula, stepping over to stand with Kevin, welcomed Larry and began with the introductions.

It's going pretty well. If only I can remember the names, thought Lawrence.

"How do you do? How do you do? Nice to meet you. Hello, nice to meet you."

Then there was Francine! She looked so very pretty in her brightly flowered dress and sandals

Paula said, "And you remember Francine, our wonderful organist."

Lawrence took Francine's hand. He blushed. She blushed. Everyone noticed and discreetly smiled and enjoyed the moment.

Look-a there! Bea thought.

Well, well! thought Anne.

Goody, goody! Paula's heart proudly jumped.

They all stood still. No one moved the least bit or even breathed.

Larry, still holding Francine's hand, softly said, "Yes, I remember. Hello, Francine."

The ladies all leaned in toward the couple to glimpse the spark that had just ignited.

Francine didn't remove her hand from Lawrence's. She stood very, very still and finally said, "Hello, Lawrence."

It was a breathless moment. Time stood still. It was totally providential. No one could have stopped it!

Everyone remembers that it was a beautiful summer evening. The meal was delicious, and the quilt was beautiful, but they will tell the story forever as the evening the Lord chose to give two of His own the gift of love.

And now, on this wintry Sunday in February at the Church of Hope, the couple had pledged their wedding vows before God. They had chosen the "love chapter" from II Corinthians of the Holy Bible to be read: *"Love is patient, love is kind . . ."*

It was just as Beatrice had predicted, and the congregation of West Hope Church and friends and family witnessed a beautiful beginning to a beautiful and long-awaited marriage.

5

The Family Portrait

When Janine and John arrived at their destination that day, they saw that Deb and Bob were already there. Deborah was the youngest of the three children. She and her husband made a very handsome couple. They were both in great shape and well matched in character and in preferences.

They bounded over to meet John and Janine, but Prince, a Black Lab, beat them to it.

"Mom, Dad, it's just so good to see you. It seems like ages," said Deborah. They all hugged one another and, arm in arm, walked into the house where the granddaughters and Kathy and Greg were waiting. Prince was as excited as the rest of the family.

Greg took the coats and hung them on the hall tree in the entry, and everyone naturally navigated toward the fireplace. They all agreed that nothing was better than the open fireplace on a brisk wintry day.

Karen and Meghan were happy to see their grandparents, as usual, and began chatting all about school and their activities.

They all eventually sat down on the comfortable furniture surrounding the fireplace.

Kathy and Greg had bought their dream home three years ago, and Kathy was quickly hired as a third-grade teacher at the area's public school. Greg had worked for years as a chemical analyst for a dairy nearby, and the move actually positioned him closer to his job.

Kathy's dream was a log home and Greg's was a commercially equipped kitchen, so after they moved in, they completely renovated the kitchen the way "The Chef" wanted it. It had commercial ovens, a gas cooking stove, a large refrigerator, and a large freezer. The entire center of the room was a working countertop with its own sink. The family benefited greatly from Greg's love for cooking. He enjoyed nothing more than to have everyone over for dinner, picnics, lunches, and even brunches. They were all considerably spoiled not having to think much about cooking anymore, but there were no complaints from anyone in that regard.

The house sat on a slight knoll at the very end of their driveway and had been beautifully landscaped, utilizing many original trees that were in harmony with the natural presentation of the house. There were rhododendron and azalea bushes bordering the driveway, which looked beautiful in whites and pinks in the summertime. There were birdbaths and feeders, and they all enjoyed watching the birds in all seasons. The house was certainly their dream come true.

The great room was aptly named, easily containing a huge six-piece curving sofa in front of the fireplace, a loveseat near the high window, various chairs and tables, a piano, and cupboards.

The wood floors were splashed with colorful rugs, and Kathy had decorated the walls with pictures of family members, some of her needlepoint, and other collections. All in all, it was warm and cozy and a very special place to be.

Greg said, "Can I get you a cup of coffee?"

Janine and John were quick to respond yes to that! "How's the practice, Bob?" John asked.

"We're busy, but better organized since Nancy came on with us. She's a gem. The best receptionist I could ever ask for. I didn't realize what a difference someone could make in the flow of the day. Ethel was a dear lady, and I hated to see her go, but I guess she needed to find something else to do that was better suited to her abilities now that she's seventy-two." "You'd get such a kick out of her now," Deborah said.

"I heard she is one of the most active members of the senior citizens group in her neighborhood, planning all sorts of events. She does enjoy life, and it's really great that she has more time to have some fun, I say. And Bob actually gets home in time for dinner now, believe it or not."

"So what does Nancy do that's so different?" asked Janine. "Oh, my goodness. She doesn't let anyone come in to sell something to me without a prior appointment, for one thing. It used to be that every time I walked down the hall, a drug salesman was following me to show me the latest medicines. Also, Nancy schedules patients more realistically, giving me the time I need and time the patient needs for a thorough exam or whatever is necessary. She seems to know just about how long a patient will be there for any sort of ailment. It reduces the stress some."

"I know that means a lot to you, Bob. You are very sincere and caring. Patients love that about you," said Janine.

"And, Deb, how is the semester coming along? Have you completed the plans for your trip to France with your students?" Deborah taught high-school French in Pittsburgh and had planned a student visit to France each year for the past few years. She and Bob had journeyed back and forth at least twice during the year. They fell in love with the Parisian culture and were fortunate to negotiate a fantastic deal to purchase a small apartment of their own in Paris. They keep it in the hands of a realtor for rental income, which in the long run has helped to make the payments for them.

Two years ago, Deborah and Bob insisted on taking Janine and John over to spend some time traveling and staying in their neat little flat. Janine was not sure about traveling out of the country, but her family knew all the safe places, and it turned out to be a trip of a lifetime for them. Now when they hear of Deborah's experiences with her students, they can follow the scenery, the cities, and the regions in their minds.

"We'll be leaving on Maundy Thursday." She began to sing, *"I love Paris in the springtime,"* and the family smiled at her imitation of a silver-screen French woman. Her excitement came through to everybody.

"Mother, Deb and I have some exciting news," said Kathy. "Okay," said Janine. She had some news too, but it could wait. She didn't actually consider her news "exciting."

"Do you want to tell them, Deb?" "No, no, Kathy. You go ahead."

"Well, Debbie has arranged for us to have a foreign exchange student from France for the month in July. She is fifteen years old from Orleans. We've wanted to do this, but we thought it would be better all the way around if Karen and Meghan were a little older. Karen's doing well with French at school, and Deb is going to help me with a refresher course. I hope I remember enough from my high school classes to be able to communicate, but Deb assures me that Claire is fluent in English. It should be a great experience for us as well as give her an opportunity to see America."

"I'm sure it will work out just great," said John. "Debbie has told us so many wonderful stories about the relationships and shared knowledge between these students and their home families. Knowledge is a huge step to understanding and cooperation between peoples."

"We're going to write a letter to Claire to tell her all about us and how happy we are that she is coming," Karen said.

"Yes, and I'm going to give her my bedroom, and Karen is going to let me sleep in her room with her. She'll love the loft and Prince, and the Fourth of July!" Meghan said.

"She sure will," said Deb. "She'll share in the celebrations of the birth of this nation, and then you all can help her celebrate Bastille Day on the fourteenth. I think July is a perfect month to have a French student come to America."

Greg brought in the coffee. "We'll see if my French cooking gets a passing grade. But she'll want some hamburgers, hot dogs, and homemade apple pie, I'm sure."

"What else is going on in the big city of Pittsburgh?" Janine asked.

"Oh boy! Busy, busy. The symphony is going strong, so I'm involved in that. The Art Association will be welcoming many artists to the annual art show in the spring. I'll be helping to plan as much as I can before leaving for France. Oh, we're going to the formal dance for the hospital fundraiser in late April. I'm trying to talk Bob into a new tux, but he's sure his will fit just fine by then," said Deborah.

"Ha! And it will! Don't worry about me. You have enough to worry about finding that perfect dress, and gloves, and shoes, and jewelry. There's a major venture."

John spoke up. "Greg, is everything under control in the kitchen? If you can sit down for a few minutes, Janine and I would like to talk with all of you about something."

"Sure." Greg sat down beside the girls. Prince immediately moved over to be close to them. They all had become very attentive.

"Well, last Thursday, I and many others at the plant were laid off permanently in a move by the board to save the company money and get it out of the red."

Everyone was waiting for John to say something more. They heard and understood what he said, but were shocked and didn't know how to respond.

Finally, Deborah spoke up. "Daddy, what are you saying? Did you lose your job?" "Yep. Exactly."

"Oh my gosh. Did you know this was going to happen, Dad?" Kathy asked.

Everyone in the room was totally focused upon John with an occasional glance at Janine to perceive her feelings if possible. The daughters were obviously shaken, and Greg and Robert seemed quite stunned.

"There had been talk of reducing the workforce, but I never dreamed they would be cutting those who had been there for as many years as I have. One thing I have learned is that seemingly no one is indispensable. It saves more money to boot us older guys out because we naturally have had pay increases over the years to garner more income. But I'll tell you . . . the company is going to find itself in a real mess working with less-experienced personnel. Well, they didn't ask me my opinion, anyway. All they wanted to do was get it over with."

"Are you saying you left that day never to return?" asked Greg.

"He came home with a box of his personal things. They gave him a box, at least," said Janine.

Deborah was getting angry as she stood. "Well, wasn't that big of them? But, Dad, the basic question now is what will you do? You are not even of retirement age, so you can't collect Social Security . . . and what about your pension? Will you lose that?"

"Actually, I don't have any answers at this time. There is going to be a meeting about the benefits available for all those released. I'm supposed to receive some word about that this week, I guess. Look. Maybe I'll even get another job."

No one seemed enthusiastic about that premise. After all, Dad was not of an age any employer would jump to hire, but they didn't say so.

"Your mother and I can survive on the securities we have, so we don't want any of you to worry one bit about this. We'll be fine. I'm just going to put it all in God's hands."

Janine spoke up. "We really haven't had time to process this new situation yet, but we will keep you informed every step of the way. That's why we came here today. We wanted to be completely honest with you."

Robert said, "Please promise us one thing more. If you need anything—anything at all—you will tell us . . . My goodness! Heaven knows how much you have given of yourselves and even of monetary advances to help all of us out over the years. John, you know we will never, ever let you lose your home, or anything else for that matter."

Oh dear! John and Janine were thinking. *Now they think we're going to go under financially.*

"Robert, really, we will be okay. I'll just have to find enough to do to stay out from under Janine's feet. She is one busy gal. Always has been. But, like I said, we have put money away for a rainy day, and so we'll draw into that as we have to. No problems, but thanks. I know you mean it, and we appreciate your love and concern."

"Let's just all stop worrying now, okay?" Janine asked. "We've told you everything, anyway. Greg, do you need some help in the kitchen?"

"Yes, I do. Come on, it's about time to pull everything together, and you are just the one I'd want to do that."

They went on into the kitchen, the children went up to the loft to watch television, and the others sat in the great room watching the fire in the fireplace.

Deborah was remembering the fortune that her parents had spent on her very fancy wedding and reception. They could now have thousands more dollars in the bank. *And what about that trip to France they financed for me upon graduating from college? I was inconsiderate . . . I was! I should have thought ahead to these days. I was selfish and hadn't thought of my parents at all. Now what?*

Kathy wanted to pray. What should I pray for? God doesn't want us to pray for someone not to go bankrupt. Isn't that wrong? If Dad is putting this all in God's hands, then I have to pray for God to hold him in His hands. That's better. That's what I'll do. *"Father in Heaven, please take care of my daddy. He's such a good man and has always given much more than was necessary to his family."* She fought back tears. She didn't want her dad to see her cry. She got up and stirred the fire and stood there for a moment, collecting her emotions.

John watched both of them. He knew they were troubled. He was sorry that they had to feel that way. But he had been troubled too, when it was new to him. It was natural. They will all feel better when they see that he and their mother were getting along as usual, except he was going to be doing something else, that's all.

Robert had picked up a magazine and was pretending to be very interested in some article. He didn't have the slightest idea what was on that page. He was thinking of John and Janine. He hoped that they understood how sincere he was about his offer to help out in any way. And he was also thinking about how many patients he had seen who had heart attacks following a traumatic event such as the loss of a job. Many had gone into depression. John was such a robust man, in great health. He wanted to say something to him about looking out for his health, but decided that if he did it could work in the reverse of what he had in mind, so he kept silent on that.

No one spoke of the job loss again that evening, but it was on everyone's mind.

John and Janine left first, and of course, the four others talked for quite some time about how they would see to it that John had things to do and that he and Janine would live a normal life far into old, old age.

"Well, that was harder than I expected," John said as they were driving home. "But you know what? They'll be fine when they have seen the proof that we are getting along well for ourselves."

"I know. They are juggling many responsibilities right now. I think they felt that they were going to have to keep us afloat. And they would do it too. Hopefully, it will never come to that. And you're right, they just need a little time to realize that they won't have to include us into their daily concerns," Janine said. "Let's not call Harry tonight. I think we've had enough for one day, don't you?"

"I agree."

6

The Western Front

Harry had been excited for John when he was told the news. His perspective—unlike the girls'—was so different. Retirement for him seemed an eternity away and something that would be wonderful in his life. He often said he would have to work to the age of seventy to put his boys through college.

He and the boys did many things together, which filled his life with great joy; but working long hours, maintaining the house and property, and finding quality time to spend with the family was challenging and frequently exhausting.

"Hey, Dad, maybe you'll come out and spend some time with us and we can clear some more of the land. And I've been thinking about that other building I need to put up for the ever-mounting stockpile of tools I've gathered. Rhonda calls them 'boys' toys,' but I do use them around here."

"Well now, there's something I definitely will place high on my list, Harry. Fresh air, hard work, and being there with you guys would be the ticket to a great escapade for me. And thanks for your viewpoint. I'll let you know how it might work out."

Janine just smiled when John told her what Harry had said. "That's Harry for you. He doesn't see in black and white. There are beautiful colors in his life, and he'll follow the rainbow to the end. I think you should go whenever he can find the free time to do the things he's talking about. You know how much you love working with Harry, John."

"When could you go, Janine?"

"Oh, honey, I can't imagine myself going this time. Lord knows when I could get away, and I wouldn't want to hold you up. You should go. Please . . . It would be good for you and Harry, and I'll make plans to go out with you some other time. Okay?"

She was working just as hard today as she did as a young woman, never thinking of slowing down and smelling the roses. There would be time enough for that later. As for now, she'd dig in—preferring the rut, the tight schedules, and the challenges of getting it all done on time and just right.

"You know what they say: 'All work and no play—'"

"I know, John. Things won't always be this way. I need a little time to adjust to a different schedule. I can't suddenly drop everything I'm doing and the plans I have made. Please try to understand. I'll work on it. I promise."

John wished that she had said "Great, let's do it," but he knew how she was, and he was used to her having to work around a full schedule. If she were going to leave town, she'd have to have time to reschedule everything. Well, it used to be the same with him, after all. He's still not exactly footloose and fancy free, but he was beginning to feel that he could adjust in a very short time. Harry had it right. Retirement could be wonderful.

7

Benefits?

The meeting hall was crowded with the recently laid-off personnel of the company. Most of the spouses were along to hear what the management had to say also. Janine actually revised her schedule to go along with John, and he was pleased that she could do that.

The meeting was very well organized, with tables of information from various insurance companies and other tables with pension and income charts and explanations of benefits. When everyone was seated, statements were made from the executives, followed by a time for questions. All the troublesome questions that most of the parties had were answered—not entirely to their complete satisfaction, but shockingly, it was not as bad as they feared.

The company would compensate the lost earnings comparable with the amount of income expected from Social Security until the discharged person reached the age of sixty-two, at which time the former employee would be responsible to either file for Social Security or seek other means of income.

As for health benefits, each person would be responsible for choosing the plan that would be best suited to the needs of the family. The company would pay a portion of the cost of each plan in line with the best offer the various companies had provided.

John gathered up all the information, heard the answers to questions he and others had asked, and they headed out through the doors. Outside of the building there were clusters of people standing around discussing the results of the meeting. Some felt abused and degraded, and others accepted their fate. It all came down to the preparations each individual had made for his own future and, consequently, how much help each felt they needed. John talked with a few of his friends. Most of them were able to resign themselves to this new situation and were discussing what they might be doing from now on. They vowed to stay in touch as people often do when parting company, and the crowd thinned as each went on his way.

John and Janine sat in the car looking over the papers for a little while before driving on home. John said, "Well, it's not too bad. The cost of insurance seems pretty high, but not totally out of reach. I've talked with some people about what they pay for health insurance, and if you aren't in a plan with a company, it can be outrageous. So I'm glad to see that we will still be on the company plan even though they aren't assuming the bulk of the cost anymore. It looks like we'll not have to draw upon our retirement investments as much as we thought. We should be quite thankful that, financially, we are still going to be okay—not flush, of course, but at the least, it will be manageable."

"You know, when Gerald was handed a forced retirement, the company sold him and the others out. There was no regard for him at all," said Janine. "That company only wanted to move ahead, and they flushed those poor employees down the drain. At least, Bilton Company didn't do that. I must say I'm relieved and maybe a bit surprised."

"Me too, I guess. I hadn't figured on much from them, so I'll not be complaining. The Lord is watching over us, and even in this instance, we've come through without too much damage. Let's not forget that he's working *His Plan*. I wonder what's next? I'm looking forward to finding out."

"John, our lives are good, don't you think? I mean what more can we do?" Janine asked.

"Only God knows. Let's get on home."

8

Easter Preparations

In West Hope, Harriet was teaching the Sunday-school class as best she could. More visiting was going on today than usual, but she understood. Most of the members, she included, were alone all week in their various houses, and coming to church on Sunday was the highlight of the week for them. They had some catching up to do. They were talking about Easter coming next week.

"Are you going to your son's for Easter, Bea?" asked Anne Kendrick.

"They were talking about coming for me. I suppose I'll go. I love to be with the family, but Easter is one of my favorite times to be at church here. I'd just love for them to come to my house instead. We'll see," she answered. "How about you?"

"Oh, we'll be here. Owen wouldn't want to miss. Some of the family will be in, and we'll go over to Alexandra's for dinner."

"That'll be nice," Julia said. "Jenny and I were talking about it just the other day. We'll both be here without family this year, so we're going to fix something between us, not that the food matters much."

Laura Davidson said, "Julia and Jenny, you two come to my house for dinner! I won't take no for an answer. My entire family of thirty some are coming for Easter. We'll have more food than we can possibly eat, and it will be really nice to have you with us."

Laura and Edward had been married for nearly sixty years, and they had spent their lives raising children and cattle. They were blessed to have their family come "home" to the farm often, especially for holidays and special occasions. Some of the family members lived within miles and could stop in often. Everyone who knew the Davidsons thought of them as the storybook-type farm family—and they were!

Julia looked at Jenny, and Julia said, "What time?"

Laura said, "We don't usually eat before two o'clock because the children always hunt for eggs around the farm first. It's such fun to watch them, so I encourage you to come as soon as you feel you want to and be a part of it."

Jenny said, "That would be nice. What do you say, Julia?" "I think that's a wonderful invitation. Thank you, Laura.

We'll come."

Iola asked, "Laura, who does the cooking for that big crowd?"

"Everybody pitches in and brings food. My daughter came up last week from Statesville. She's such a help, and I'll bake the pies on Saturday."

Everyone knows that Laura's pies are the best. Her secret is that she uses lard in the crust. Even though most of her friends and neighbors never use lard themselves, they eat her pies without hesitation.

Laura's husband had not been feeling especially well the past week or so. He couldn't keep up with all the work around the farm and had to have help for the first time in his eighty-plus years. Laura always did help with the work, but she might possibly be doing a lot more for a while. There had been talk of selling the cattle, but so far it was just talk. It would be a sad day if it happened.

"Will you have the family in, Iola?" asked Harriet.

"Oh yes. They are coming. I'll be cooking it all myself, which is fine with me. They'll not be here before three o'clock as they are staying home to go to their own churches. I get to do Easter. It's the only holiday I have. All the others are distributed around, so I make the most of it and enjoy the cooking and the fussing. I always did."

"And you do a fantastic job of it too. Every time our Women's Association comes for the annual dinner, your table is set so beautifully, and we are treated to an outstanding dinner," said Adele.

Adele's daughter would be home for Easter. She had been excited about that for several weeks. Her daughter Mildred lived in the Midwest and didn't often get "home" for holidays. The class knew she was truly looking forward to her visit.

"Well, the church music is going to be special, I'll bet. Francine has been so happy lately, and do you notice how it comes out in her music? She seems to be raising the decibels on the organ too, as though she just can't hold back," said Anne.

"That's for sure! I can't control my hearing aid sometimes. When she turns the organ up, I have to turn my hearing aid down in a hurry or it seems my brains will be blown out," said Iola. She had so much trouble with adjusting her hearing aid just right. It was always too loud, or she couldn't hear much of anything.

"I like it," said Julia. "I do too," said Anne.

"Alice told me that Francine and Larry want to move to Florida, at least during the winter months. I guess Larry had already bought a piece of property and a house before he met Fran, and now they both want to go," Bea said.

"Why don't they?" asked Jenny.

"Well, you know how dedicated Francine has been to Hope Church with the music, and she just can't bring herself to leave the church without an organist," Bea responded.

"Can't we just get another organist?" asked Julia.

"I guess you can hardly find an organist these days. Francine says it takes years of lessons and practice, and today's young people want instant gratification, not years of preparations," said Bea.

"Iola, why can't you play the piano for services until we can find someone else? Surely, there's someone out there," said Laura.

"I can't do that anymore. It makes me too nervous. I haven't spent much time at the piano for years, and I could never get back what I've lost now. It would not be possible." It was obvious that no one was going to change her mind on that!

"Well, then what? Maybe if the session would advertise in the paper or something? Some churches do that. Look how long Fran has served in this church. She certainly deserves some happiness with her new husband," said Adele, who was always looking out for everyone to feel good about themselves—anytime, anywhere.

"She does, but she'd feel a lot better if she knew it was what the Lord wants her to do, so she has spoken to the session about it, and I guess she asked them to pray for the Lord to provide a replacement if it is His will. She's not going to go until she knows that. That's what I heard," said Bea.

Harriet said that's the way it should be. "We should all turn to the Lord for the right answers and do our best to live according to His purpose, whatever it is."

They all agreed.

The bell rang to end the class, and they dismissed with prayer and went on into the sanctuary.

9

He Is Risen!

Kathy, Greg, and the girls came back to Center Church in Innesport for Easter, as did many others. The church was filled from back to front, which was extraordinary—especially for the pews in the front. The family missed not seeing John in church this morning, but was pleased that he went out to visit Harry and the boys. They could only imagine the good times they all were having together. It's hard to be separated by so many miles from those you love, but Harry tried to shorten the vast, empty space with visits and telephone calls as frequently as possible.

Easter was Janine's favorite Sunday of the year—the day the Lord had made for all as the day of salvation. She wanted to praise Him with all that she had, and what she had was music. The compositions for this day were the finest, and she would play them to His glory the best she could.

She usually played a longer prelude on Easter because the congregation was more tolerant and appreciative of the music on this day than on any other. Instead of the usual chatter during the prelude, most of the people actually listened and were glad to be in the house of the Lord.

Pastor Jim was uplifted by the attendance and wished the flock felt the overwhelming desire to praise the Lord every Sunday. He would not complain. Someone out there would receive a message today that God had called him to hear, and Jim would be the one to deliver it. He was happy for the glorious message of the resurrection to expound upon this morning.

Janine played J. S. Bach's "Jesu, Joy of Man's Desiring" first of all, and then a resounding composition with trumpets and full organ. If she had turned up the volume any louder, the chandelier would have begun to sway; but the congregation had come to celebrate, and the music was totally appropriate.

Pastor Jim called the congregation to worship: "He is risen!"

The response echoed: "He is risen, indeed!"

The service was as it always had been—joyful and full of praise. Kathy moved into the choir to sing the "Hallelujah Chorus" from Handel's *Messiah*. The choir director had invited Kathy to do so as she knew the alto part as well as anyone in the choir. The congregation stood, and all participants and the congregation were overjoyed with it.

Janine played a Bach *toccata* with everything she had left in her. She would be exhausted from this day, but delightfully so. Easter was the objective of a long, long season of practice and preparation for any church musician and the highlight of the year.

Janine hurried home to change her clothes. Even though the girls were growing up, they still wanted to have an Easter egg hunt—so, needless to say, Janine wanted to be there to enjoy that event with the family.

She missed John. She felt no guilt for not going with him after being at church today, but she had felt his absence, and it seemed strange without him. They both loved Easter.

Even though she should hurry along, she could not resist driving around through West Hope. As she did, she read the church sign: "HE IS RISEN! HALLELUJAH!"

That's right, she thought. And that's what it's all about!

"He lives, He lives," she sang as she turned onto McDade Road, rejoicing in this most significant day of all days.

As she drove along, she saw that there was a "For Sale" sign on one of the houses.

Isn't that a nice-looking house? And it's sitting on a lovely piece of property. I wonder why they would want to sell? Very nice. She drove on past.

ϓϓϓ

The day was warm, and so were their hearts of the family members as they shared in the celebration. The girls clambered for each egg, running back and forth and having a laughingly good time. They sat down to a delicious dinner of lamb, complained about eating too much, and were filled with satisfaction and familiar conversations.

Janine spent the night as planned as Meghan moved on over to Karen's room. She looked around the room, which was in soft pinks with ruffled white window curtains, and remembered how she loved fussing with the little-girl rooms in her own family. Meghan's room wasn't really much different—she had a shelf of dolls, lots of stuffed animals, and a bookcase with classic and non-classic literature, as she was an ardent reader. There was a music system of some sort and, unlike her mother's old room at Janine's home, a computer and printer. Of course, in today's world, the computer is as important as the typewriter or a set of encyclopedias would have been to the generation before. Life moves on.

She loved the softness and innocence of the room and felt very comfortable to be staying the night.

Karen and Meghan joined her on the bed for a while. Janine loved having the girls near to her, and they talked with her about the things that were on their minds.

Karen was bursting with excitement that she had a part in the school's musical production. "I will be a member of a group of girls who are in almost every scene. I even have two lines to sing all by myself."

"Well, that's terrific. Those voice lessons are paying off, aren't they?"

"I guess so. By the time I'm a senior, I hope I'll have a much bigger part."

"I'm sure you will, Karen. You've worked hard at your music training. Keep at it."

"I will. I know I haven't had much time lately to practice the piano, Grandma, but I want to get back to lessons as soon as school is out. Will that be okay with you?"

"Absolutely! We'll do it. I'm so happy to teach you, honey. You have been doing a lot on the piano this year at chorus, which has helped you to keep at it. Now back to exercises and scales."

Janine laughed as Karen scowled. She grabbed her and rolled on the bed with her as they had done together since the girls were toddlers. Meghan eagerly joined in with a squeal, and they all loved just touching and being close.

Grandma needed to catch her breath, so they calmed down for a moment.

"And little Ms. Meghan, what are you going to do all summer? Are you ready to try the piano?"

"I don't think so. Mom has taught me a little bit, but I'd rather dance."

"That's good too, but you should give some instrument a try."

"Oh, I'm going to. I want to play the drums!" "The drums?"

"Yes, I'm going to learn at school, and also the violin." "Meghan, you are one big surprise! Go for it, girl!"

They resumed their romp, and Kathy peeked in to see what all the noise was about. Prince had come with her, and before anyone could think, he was in the mix.

The exercise was enough to put Grandma into exhaustion, but she loved every minute of it. What a joy having grandchildren!

Kathy scooted everyone out of Grandma's room and hugged her mother, and soon all was quiet in the house.

Janine slept deeply from exhaustion and also from the comfort of a good day with loved ones.

ϓϓϓ

The next morning, after a small breakfast, she and Kathy decided to take a walk. Prince could hardly contain himself. He ran to the left of the road and sniffed into the trees, came back out and walked a bit with the women, then moved to the right and sniffed. He was on a discovery mission to find out if any new animals had moved in. Kathy called him back from a rabbit chase and poured some of her bottled water into a scout pan that she carried for him. All three of them were enjoying the exercise.

"How long has it been since anyone has spotted a bear around here?"

"Oh, Mother, don't worry about that. The lane was named Bear Track because of the Indians, probably two hundred years ago. I guess the bears were tracked in this area, but after the settlers came in the late 1700s, the bears were driven out or pretty much killed off. There were stories of the early settlers being attacked for a few years, though. Those must have been very difficult times. God bless them. How they ever survived in the wilderness with so little, I'll never know."

"Not only did they survive the elements and the wild animals, but the Indians did not actually welcome them, either. Now, we can walk safely and not worry about a thing."

They turned from the lane onto McDade Road. There still was not much traffic to bother them.

They passed the neighbors sitting on the porch of the old farmhouse, and they waved. Kathy said she hadn't actually met them yet, but they were always friendly. Daffodils were blooming, and touches of green grass could be seen in the yard. The couple on the porch was anticipating the arrival of the first robins and the budding of the trees. Winters were long for the farmers, and yearly revival of the land brought movement and hope as the pulse of the earth greatly affected all God's creatures.

How quiet it was. Janine forgot that Kathy was with her for a moment as she became lost in her own thoughts. In the countryside, one could easily forget how engaged and crazy the world had truly become. Few in the city would be thinking of spring. More likely, attention would be on those maddening end-of-the-year reports, children's programs and recitals, and shopping for a new season's wardrobe.

Here, the new wardrobe would be green grass and flowering meadows. The new fragrance would not come from Estée Lauder or Ralph Lauren, but rather from apple blossoms, honeysuckle, and freshly mown hay.

Why am I thinking this way? I'm certainly not longing for the rural life. The city has always been the life for me with symphonies, great stores, international restaurants, and such; and I never want to be far removed from all of that. When did I ever even think about honeysuckle and apple blossoms before?

Their walk continued past the little country church that Kathy had been attending. She said perhaps twenty to twenty-five people belonged there. It felt cozy to her, and she was helping out by playing the hymns on the piano. The church was of painted wood, sitting up on a high foundation, and had a small yet old cemetery behind it. It obviously had been there for the neighborhood for a long time.

"What did they do for music here yesterday?" Janine asked.

"A young woman who is a college student was going to be home with her family, and she planned on providing the piano music. She was always dependable in that manner as she was growing up. I'm sure the congregation enjoyed having her back on the bench, so to speak."

Before long, they came to the house with the "For Sale" sign in front. It looked as though the owners were not at home. Janine pointed out to Kathy that the house was for sale and asked if she knew the people who lived there.

"I haven't seen anyone here lately. I think they have already moved. I see that Crisscross Realty is handling it for them. I did hear that the lady of the house became very ill, and the husband couldn't keep up. That's always a shame."

"It's a fine-looking home," said Janine. "I wonder if we might walk around the back. I'm sure no one is here."

"Okay. Let's go look."

The ranch-style home had a full-sized basement that opened up to the outside from the back to a nice patio. The yard had been neatly kept—perhaps an acre with an apple tree, several maple trees, a grape arbor, other bushes and shrubs, and a separate garage. The property seemed to end at the wooded area down behind.

"Well, this is really nice," said Kathy.

"It is!" They began to feel like intruders, and so they went back to the road and turned back to the house.

"Grandma, Grandma," called Karen. "Granddad just called. He said maybe you could call him this morning. They would not be going outside today until later. He and Uncle Harry were drawing up something inside. I don't know what."

Janine smiled. "Thanks, honey. I'm going to be getting along home very shortly. I'm having a meeting at my house this week, and there are things to be done. I'll call Granddad from there."

She wished she hadn't volunteered to be host. She should have known that she'd need a few days to unwind and rest after Easter. Oh well. She'd do what she must. Maybe she'd take a tiny little nap this afternoon before she thought any more about the meeting.

"Meghan, thank you for sharing your room with me last night. I slept very well. I can't believe how quiet it was—no cars going by and no sirens in the night. I said my prayers, turned out the light, and listened. The silence seemed to cover me with peace somehow. It was so very nice."

"You're welcome, Grandma. Anytime you come, you just figure on using my room. Okay?"

"Okay," she said.

10

Picture This!

Janine resisted the temptation to once again take the longer way home through West Hope because she was eager to get home and call John and she also had a number of things on her list to do today.

She was soon on the highway, and there weren't as many trucks on the road today, the day after Easter. *Many truckers had one extra day off to enjoy with their families,* Janine decided.

She pulled into the garage and gathered her bag and purse. As soon as she made a pot of coffee, she dialed Harry's phone number. Rhonda answered the phone.

"Oh, Janine, it's you. Great. Hey, boys, it's Grandma. We've missed you. Little James can't understand where you are. He expects you and Granddad to be together."

"I'm sure they are having a great time with Granddad, but he's probably having a better time than anyone."

"I don't know about that, but it's been fun. How was Easter at your church?"

"Wonderful! I love Easter, as you know. I confess that I missed John, but with Kathy and her family there, it was good.

We all had a fine day. You should have seen the girls rushing to get the largest amount of eggs. It was fun. I hope they never tire of doing it. Did you all get to church?"

"Of course. We dressed up our little cowboys in their best boots and bejeweled shirts. They really looked spiffy. I'll send you pictures. Here's John. I'll get the boys on in a bit."

"Okay. Thanks, sweetie."

"Hi, babe," said John. "So, did you have a nice walk this morning?"

"Yes, I did. The daffodils are blooming, and the countryside is turning green. It was very peaceful and such a nice place to walk. No trucks and no loud noises—only the soft mooing of the cows and an occasional bark of a dog in the distance . . . Very nice."

"I'm glad. I'm really enjoying the outdoors here, but we've been making some noise of our own with the chainsaw while expanding the open areas up a bit. The boys are going to have lots of room to run here in the yard. It's about the size of a soccer field now."

"John, are you drinking lots of water and getting a rest now and then?"

"Now, now, don't you worry about me. Rhonda keeps a check on that. She sends water out to us in thermos jugs. William brings it out with his wagon, sometimes pulling Charles and James too. They are a big help and such happy little guys. They keep me smiling, for sure."

She smiled also as she envisioned a "Norman Rockwell" type picture of the three boys and the wagon.

"Janine, are you there?" John asked.

"Oh yes. Sorry. How's Harry? Did he get the time off work, then?"

"Oh yes. He took some vacation time. The company is good about it all, and told him to use more time this week if he wants to. We've called a friend of his who does excavation to come over and dig us out a section for the toolshed. Well, Harry calls it a toolshed. I'd call it a big old storage garage. After it gets dug out, we'll start laying the blocks together. He wants to help me set those, as he knows he's better at that than I am. That'll take the biggest part of this week, we figure. Next week, I can measure and cut boards for the building while he's at work, and we can put them up together in the evenings. Rhonda said she'd help, and I believe she can. She's quite the partner for Harry."

"Well, sounds like you have some more work to do. Don't rush yourself. I can manage, and you know I'll keep myself busy. I'm happy for Harry and the boys that you are there. Just take care of yourself. Okay?"

"I will. Well, the boys are all lined up to talk with you, so I'll say good-bye. I love you."

"I love you too," she said with a tinge of sadness and longing to have him home, but she would not say anything about that.

Janine talked to each one of the boys. They went on and on about Granddad and Daddy cutting down trees and how they were helping carry branches into the woods and stacking up wood for the winter. She wished she could see that! They were so sweet and dear to her and were going to grow up without her seeing it happen.

She told them all she loved them. They all told her that they loved her too. She hung up the phone and stared into space for a long time.

"Time waits for no one," the old saying goes. It surely doesn't. It really rushes past sometimes. Harry was a little boy a few years ago, wasn't he? Now he has three boys of his own. She sat there thinking of Harry as a youngster and what a joy he always was to his parents. Everyone loved Harry.

"*I'm just wild about Harry, and Harry's wild about me.*" She started to sing the song in her head. She had a song for everything. Not everyone in the family appreciated her breaking into song all the time. They would never know how many times she kept the songs to herself so as not to see their raised eyebrows, but she would always have the music and songs—at least, for herself.

Her thoughts continued on and on until, suddenly, she realized she had been thinking there for a half hour. *Time is rushing by right now!* She hurried into her office to gather up some devotional books from one of the shelves.

11

Out of Focus

The meeting will be Thursday, and I said I'd give the devotions for Arlene. I think I'd better try to get that settled.

I can't even think of what kind of devotion to do. I'm still tired from Sunday. I know I slept well last night, but I think I'm totally exhausted; nevertheless, I'd better get started on this. First, I need to calm down. I need to focus on a prayer and a scripture or something.

She couldn't do it. Her mind was whirling. She felt left out by not going to Oklahoma, but how could she go? Well, she could have. John was perfectly willing to go after Easter, but with Harry requesting last week off, it seemed better that John go ahead when he did.

She mustn't forget to call the church tomorrow to reserve the chapel for the piano recital of her two students. They were the only two left to her teaching. She had not taken on any new students for a few years, anticipating retirement.

Retirement? Ha ... That's a laugh. I'll never retire. I don't have enough sense to retire. Could I be happy traveling without any responsibilities like some of my friends are doing? I know that I'd never, ever be satisfied doing that.

She started going from room to room, meandering, eventually turning on the television. She didn't normally enjoy it, but she occasionally found it entertaining. She turned the dials to get some news. Nothing of interest seemed to be happening. At least, there were no bombings or anything like that. She turned it off. She had things she should be doing, anyway.

She thought of the nice house for sale on McDade Road. *I could enjoy living there,* she thought.

What? I'm losing my mind. Why did I even think of that? I have a very, very full life right here! I am never moving! My goodness!

She went back to look through the books of devotionals, and while she was leafing through them, the telephone rang.

"Allô, mère! Comment allez-vous?"

"Deborah! I'm fine. How are you? Is everything all right?"

"Absolutely. The students are getting settled into their rooms. Our luggage arrived with us, thank heavens, and the trip over went well. You should have seen everyone as they came into Paris International. It's always the same, and yet ever exciting to be with them and share their new experiences. I just wanted you to know we're here and give you a telephone number in case you need to call. I know you won't, but just in case."

"Well, fine. That's great. Did you call Robert?"

"Yes, I did."

"Okay. So you'll be two weeks, right?"

"Right. That's not much time, really, as you know, but we will hit the main tourist attractions. The group can't wait to get started, and I know they will go from morning to night. We'll be dragging into Pittsburgh when we come back, but it'll be worth it. Did you have a nice Easter?"

"Oh my, yes, and I enjoyed the day with Kathy's family. We missed you and seeing you dive for the Easter eggs. But the girls had a great time. I talked with your dad just a while ago, and he's fine, enjoying the out of doors and being with Harry and the boys."

"That's good. I knew he would. Well, Mom, take care of yourself. Try not to work every minute of every day. There's more to life than constant work, you know? Oh dear, here I am preaching at you all the way from across the ocean. I'm sorry. You know I love you and mean well. Right?"

"Of course . . . I love you too. Have a great time, dear. Take the students to see the French dancers. But control yourself when you do!"

They both laughed. When she hung up, she was smiling and picturing Deborah truly in her element. She hadn't any children of her own yet, which has turned out to be a blessing for many young people as she has the time and the pleasurable energy to give so much to them.

Her students are incredibly lucky to have her for a teacher, mentor, and example.

12

Blowing in the Wind

She eventually managed to read some devotions, all the while telling herself that she didn't have all day to find the right one. The pressure was on! She went through a devotional book for women. It was fine, but not exactly right.

Come on, Janine, you don't have all day. Stop being so fussy.

She always thought those little books were particularly helpful, so what was wrong with her today? If she didn't find something soon, she'd have to resort to writing her own. She had done that for the devotions for an entire year a while back. It was a rewarding exercise as it brought her closer to the Lord. She remembered how much she loved writing about the scriptures.

That was when she was not so busy! She couldn't possibly settle down enough to do that today. She began to regret that she was in such a predicament now. Where was she going with her life? She felt under great stress and began to think she wasn't going to be able to find a devotion that would satisfy her.

I'll use one of my old ones. She stood to go to her files. *I can't do that! The women have heard all of them before.*

"Lord, when did I get myself into such a tizzy? And why am I noticing this so much now when I thought I was perfectly satisfied with everything as it is? I am satisfied! I'm doing good work. I'm doing all that I can for the church—maybe too much. Can we do too much? We can't! We have to do everything we possibly can. Well, I'm trying."

She picked up the Bible. Starting with Genesis, she read the Creation story. What a marvelous, marvelous beginning. God created everything. Of course, she knew that. He created the stars, the earth, the waters and the mountains, the animals, and finally Adam and Eve. And then He rested.

He rested.

Does this mean that God didn't work all the time? In any case, He doesn't have to work all the time. He has it all worked out.

I remember in the New Testament where Jesus left the crowd and disciples and rested at times. Jesus lived as an example to all of us, and He rested. So is it all right for us to take time off? No one had a more important job on this earth than Jesus, and He rested and retreated from it at times.

Feeling confused and very uncomfortable with her thoughts, Janine thought of one of her favorite hymns, "What a Friend We Have in Jesus," and went over it in her mind. She would take it to the Lord as the hymn said.

She prayed, asking the Lord for help in understanding the scriptures she had just read. Admitting to herself and aloud to God that she was under stress, she prayed for God to calm her and lead her in the right direction.

She was drawn to the blue book in the stack. She picked it up, ruffled through some pages, and came upon a title that intrigued her.

The Little Wind

(Read Psalm 63)

Over the waters of the South Pacific, a little breeze was born. He was gentle and mild and moved very softly.

As he grew a little, he began to truly enjoy being a breeze. He would lift and swoosh and move very lightly over the ocean. He particularly enjoyed riding on the backs of the dolphins and whales, and they seemed to enjoy having him around. They would frolic and play all day. They all began to move a little faster, turning northward, being drawn to the cooler waters.

The little breeze began to grow and grow. He grew very strong, and as he moved over the waters, he caused the waves to rise and increase and toss about.

He just couldn't control himself. He became stronger and stronger, and could move faster and faster. He turned completely away from the course he was meant to follow. When he blew across dry land, he noticed that everything under him became terribly stirred up and sometimes torn apart. He wanted to say he was sorry, but he couldn't stop long enough to do that.

He was moving along at a pace now that he did not like. It was a pace he could not manage. He was moving but accomplishing nothing worthwhile. He longed for the days when he was young, when everything seemed simple and he could rest once in a while and enjoy his life.

He tried and tried to make himself stop. He made wishes. He made promises. He squeezed everything within himself to find the control he so desperately wanted. The effort was all to no avail.

One day, he came to a sea. It was a beautiful sea, very blue and peaceful, and he wanted to stop there and rest; however, all he did was stir up the waters. Great waves formed, clouds joined him in his journey, and a terrible storm erupted. It was his fault. If only he knew how to calm himself. The stress was too much. What could he do?

He came upon a boat full of men. He could see that the boat was going to sink because of the strain he was putting upon it. He felt absolutely dreadful. A man in the boat stood. The man looked straight at him, lifted his hand, and said, "Peace. Be still." And because the man spoke with all authority of heaven and earth, the wind listened to him and stopped what he was doing and became calm.

The wind was amazed that he no longer was in a torrent of constant movement and stress. He rejoiced that he could once again be the happy little breeze he once was and realized that all of his own efforts to accomplish this were impossible without the help of the one sent by God who brought peace to him.

He would remember Him. He would turn to Him for help the next time he got himself into an uncontrollable situation. He blew gently on, came once again to the waters, and lived a peaceful and productive life doing what he was born to do.

ϒϒϒ

- Janine had read the scripture and the story and associated it with herself immediately.
- The devotion ended with a suggested discussion or a prayer. The discussion leader could ask the following questions:
- Have you ever felt that your life was out of control? If so, what did you do?
- Do you always feel it is your total responsibility to be in control of your life? If so, why?
- Do we become overwhelmed sometimes because we are following our own course instead of God's?
- Are you willing to let go of your own plans and desires to follow the path God is choosing for you?

- Janine pondered the questions and knew that she was moving along on her own and was exhausted trying to figure everything out for herself.

She read the prayer:

"Father in Heaven, be with us and help us to call upon you at all times for directions in our lives so that all we do will be for your glory. We ask this, Father, not for our own benefit, but so that we will be used to do your will as you have planned.

We pray, Father, in the name of your Son, Jesus, who has the authority to calm the storms and set us on the course we should follow. Amen."

ΎΎΎ

During the following day, Janine realized even further how important this little story was to her. It could certainly change the way she had been thinking, and it might even change the future. Was she willing to accept that? She wasn't sure, but she knew she had discovered something significant, and she would not set it aside and forget it. She decided to use the story of the little wind as her devotional for Thursday evening.

13

Is Anybody Listening?

Eighteen ladies came to the meeting, all happy to be there and talking over many things. Janine had planned well and had provided seating for everybody. After some cool drinks, they were seated for the meeting.

Janine called the meeting to order as president and then moved on to the devotions. She was especially eager to read "The Little Wind" and had practiced reading it with much emphasis. The ladies were smiling as they listened.

When she finished, someone responded, "That was sweet."

Another asked, "Was that in one of the children's books?"

"No. It really isn't a child's story. It is meant for adults . . . for us."

"Oh. Well, it was very nice," another responded.

Janine realized that no one caught the meaning. If anyone did, she certainly couldn't sense it. She said, "There are some questions for us to consider, which should help us understand the real meaning of this story. Let's go over them."

These questions will lead everyone to the right way of thinking, I hope.

The questions were hardly answered at all. Responses such as "Oh, maybe, a little," to the first question was about all she heard. The rest of the questions prompted shrugs and not much more.

She couldn't believe it! She was totally flabbergasted that no one caught on. How could this be? It was as clear as clear could be. *Were they listening, or not?* Well, she couldn't keep on the subject forever. She asked them to bow for the prayer. They did, of course, but even then she didn't think they were with her at all.

The meeting continued with the business. They heard reports, planned an upcoming event for the spring, voted to give a small check to a needy student, and discussed other important issues.

As they were preparing to conclude the business, Libby asked if she could read a nice poem by Helen Steiner Rice. Permission was granted, and she said she had found this nice poem when going through cards at the store and wanted to share it.

It was sweet and lovely, and everyone praised her for her selection and caring enough to share it with the group.

They closed with the benediction, Janine served her dessert that she had baked herself (of course), and they sat around for a while longer. She heard nothing about the devotion she had offered, but many went on and on about the poem!

When they left, she plopped down on the sofa and wanted to cry. What was wrong? She believed the devotion was pertinent and helpful, and she felt absolutely frustrated that no one else had a clue as to what the purpose of it was.

She cleaned everything up, vacuumed, put the dishes in the dishwasher, turned off the lights, and momentarily forgot the message of the little wind. She was not calm, nor was she happy—but rather in a torrent of emotions.

"Lord, why did I not reach them? I really wanted to."

She went to bed and decided to go see Pastor Jim in the morning. There were too many things she absolutely did not understand.

14

The Ladies of West Hope

"Good morning, Adele," said Beatrice. "I just got back from Ron's. What's been going on around here?"

"Good morning to you," said Adele. "I'm glad you called. You must have ESP. Mildred left for home this morning, and I'm feeling a little sad. But we had a wonderful visit, so I can't complain."

"Did you and Mildred have a good visit with Candice?" Bea asked.

"Yes, we did. We went over to the house on Saturday. Samantha had fixed a really nice lunch for us. Billie sure married a gem. Samantha had Candice all dressed up in a spring robe, and there was a beautiful bouquet of Easter flowers on the nightstand."

Bea said, "Samantha is truly a Godsend to your family, isn't she?"

"She certainly is, and she never complains about taking full care of her mother-in-law. Bea, that's a very big job, you know."

"Yes, I do know. I remember very clearly your eighteen-hour days for years after Candice had that terrible accident. That was just about the worst thing that ever happened. Not only did Candice lose her husband and pretty much her own life, but she had little Billie who couldn't take care of himself. I'll tell you, Adele, you were a saint to take them in and care for them all those years."

"Now, Bea. You would have done the same thing. We were family."

"I know, but with Candice totally unable to do for herself, you had to use every ounce of energy you had caring for her and your small grandson."

"Well, I had my husband then, and Mildred was actually quite helpful. I think it was harder on her in her teen years than on any of us. But let's get back to your visit with Ron. Did you have a nice Easter with the family?"

"Oh, I did. You know I really wanted to stay home, but Ron wouldn't let me do that. He believed that I'd be better off with the family on the holiday, and as it turned out, he sure was right. I'll tell you, those great grandbabies of mine are growin' like weeds. We had a fun time together. I showed them how to play ball. They learned a little about swingin' a bat as I pitched."

"My goodness. You pitched? I'd throw my back out doing something like that," said Adele. "I never really learned much about any kind of sport, anyway."

"Well, that's because you were brought up like a little lady. Me? I was just one of the boys being raised with all my brothers.

I didn't want to be left out, so I learned how to compete with them and even their friends. I'll tell you, I was pretty good at baseball. I'd sometimes get picked on a team real early.

"I was wondering, how did everything go on Easter?" Bea asked. "Was the service nice?"

"It was, at that. We had the early service with near to a hundred people there."

"Really?"

"Yes. Then we all stayed for the breakfast fit for a farmer. Lucy and Raymond once again cooked eggs, ham, sausage, and biscuits. Others brought in donuts of every kind, fresh fruit—you name it! It was delicious."

Bea asked, "Did you stay for the regular service, then?" "Of course! We all did, and there were about a hundred more people came in. You should've seen the memorial flowers. They were all over the floor in front of the pulpit and in every window, and there were more on some flower stands in the entry. As usual, the fragrance was powerful and almost overwhelming, but I took care of my sinuses this time. I took an allergy pill early that morning. I brought your lily home to give to you."

"Oh, thanks for taking care of that. I'll tell you, I did miss coming to my church. Easter is so special. But Ron said he'd come here next year, God willing. This year I'll be eighty-two years old, so I'm not expecting anything from one year to another any more."

"Oh, go on. You know you'll live to be a hundred. You are the youngest eighty-two-year-old I know of. Oh, before I forget, I wanted to tell you. The church is planning a softball game for the congregation later in the year—with hot dogs and hamburgers—

out at the ballpark right after church. I can't remember if I heard of a date, but it should be something to do, don't you think?"

"Something to do? I'd love it. I'm gonna sign up to pitch." "Beatrice! You'd better leave that up to the younger folks.

We can sit and cheer."

"Not me. I'm gonna play ball. I get tired of sittin' around.

A day of fun in the sun—that's for me."

"I don't see you sitting much when the weather is nice.

You work your flowers and cut your grass and such." "Harrumph! That's work. I do it to keep fit, and it's cheap!

It's not what you'd call fun, is it?"

"You seem to enjoy it. I think you should get Silas to cut your grass like I do."

"I don't want to spend my little bit of Social Security paying somebody to do what I can do myself."

"Well, would you like to come over for lunch today? I have ham left over from Easter Sunday, and I could use a little friendly visit."

"Sounds good to me. I'll be over in a while. Thanks. By the way, how's Edward Davidson? Have you heard anything?"

"Oh yes. Jenny called me yesterday to tell me that he had to go to the doctor on Tuesday. He was fine for the family get-together on Easter, and then on Monday he had a spell of some kind. His daughter Hannah was still there, and she took him. The doctor ran a few tests and wants him to get an EKG and blood test."

"Oh dear," said Bea. "Ed is getting up there. He's older than I am—I know that. Laura has always been the healthy one in the family. She's gonna have to be strong now, that's for sure. Our old friends are old, you know? It's something we're just going to have to face."

"I guess you're right. Well, come on over when you get yourself ready. I'll be here."

"All righty. See you soon."

Adele and Beatrice live near one another in West Hope, and they very much enjoy one another. They are of entirely different personalities but participate in church life together, which is about all they have left at this stage of their lives.

They are friends, and they know that friendships are as precious as anything they could claim. The others in their Sunday-school class were dear to them as well, but Bea and Adele living close had established a bond together that meant a lot to them.

Iola telephoned Julia later that day. "Hello," said Julia.

"It's Iola. Are you going to get your hair done Friday as usual?"

"Well, I guess so. I always do. Why do you ask?"

"I had my appointment moved to the morning. Actually, it is right after your appointment, which you always have. But my problem is that my car is in the garage and won't be done until Friday afternoon. I was thinking that if you could pick me up, we could go together. That is, if you wouldn't mind sitting and waiting for me to be finished."

"Well, that's fine. I'll come by for you. That won't be any problem. What's new?"

"What could be new around here? Nobody died. That's always good news. Harriet got herself a puppy."

"Oh my! I can't believe it. She travels so much. What is she going to do when she goes away?"

"Exactly! I said the same thing. She said she'd worry about it later. But for now, she is enjoying the company of the little thing. I wouldn't have one! Too much trouble, if you ask me. A puppy has to be followed around all the time if you want to protect your carpet and what have you. And you *have* to take it outside. She can't keep up with that. I told her so. She said her son lives close enough, and he said he'd take care of it when she's gone away."

"Well, that sounds like a pretty good arrangement. She's younger than we are, so I suppose she can handle it."

"It's not that I can't handle it. I could if I wanted to. I just don't want to. Did you talk with that realtor?"

"I did. He wants to buy my house and let me live in it until I die. What do you think of that?"

"You'd better get some advice on that, and watch out for someone taking you across the coals."

"I know. I don't want to sell my house, anyway. I have no intentions of it. Did he stop up there?"

"No. And he might as well not. I'm not going to talk with him about such a thing."

"I wish it would warm up some. Seems kind of cold today, don't you think?"

"Oh, not too bad. Of course, it's April. We could get any kind of weather between now and the middle of May. I'd better go. Thanks for agreeing on tomorrow. Will you be coming by around ten o'clock?"

"Yes. That's about right. See you then. Good-bye." "Good-bye."

The ladies of West Hope lived in separate houses, mostly alone. Iola, Adele, Julia, Beatrice, and Rachael all came to the community because they had married men from the immediate area, and now all five were widows. It always happened that a widow in West Hope who moved in from another place stayed put when her husband died. There are a large number of those, and many belong to the Church of Hope.

They came there during the 1930s. Life became very hard during the Depression, and they survived because they had one another. Friendships had developed, children played together, and they came to depend upon one another in the borough.

Some women lost husbands during World War II. The community of West Hope actually lost a very large percentage of men during the war. Life had been hard then, also. The friendships deepened—as they will during times of uncertainty, pain, and grief. West Hope was a community of the "best hope" in many ways.

Jenny always lived there, and Anne came to the outer community some years back. Harriet actually lived outside of the borough also, but the church in West Hope was always the church of her husband's family. In the beginning, she had no other choice, and today she would say, "Choice or no choice, this will always be the church for me."

Harriet had been the class teacher ever since the original teacher became too ill to continue. She always could be counted upon to help out in various other ways, as well.

Her husband died suddenly some years back, which automatically enrolled her into the old widows' group, although she was somewhat younger than the rest. Not that anyone *wanted* to get into that group. It has no name, isn't active in any groupie way, and doesn't meet together except on Sunday mornings.

They basically have a history that ties them together and gives them a sense of security somehow.

ᵞᵞᵞ

The sirens were sounding as the emergency vehicle passed the beauty parlor. Julia listened as it faded out of range. The beautician said, "Somebody's going to the hospital, I suppose."

Julia hated the sound. She'd heard it before, as had others in the community. If it had stopped in their community, she would know the one in the ambulance. She didn't want to have to face another loss. She valued every friend and their families. Everyone in West Hope felt the fist of anxiety push upon the chest as the sirens blew through. Everyone, that is, except Iola who was under the hairdryer with her hearing aid removed.

"Two weeks ago, it was Madelyn McKay, and she didn't ever come back."

"I know," said Julia. "I heard she had a stroke. Poor Walter. He will miss her so much. We all will."

Iola was humming a little children's song. She was smiling and remembering her young choirs of years past. When they paid the beautician and left the shop, Julia told Iola about the ambulance. They, like most everyone in the community, picked up the telephone as soon as each got home. They were saddened to learn that Edward occupied the ambulance today. He had chest pains and was taken to the hospital. Everyone who heard said a prayer for his health—and for Laura too as she faced this difficult time.

15

A "Stirring"

In the city, Janine had met with Pastor Jim and told him of her experience with the devotion the previous evening and said, "I cannot believe that not one person was moved by the story. It was so meaningful."

He smiled knowingly. "Janine, I have wondered about the same thing many times when I thought I had a significantly key message on a Sunday morning and looked out upon a sea of blank faces. You see, the Holy Spirit moves us to hear, but we have a choice to make. We can open up our hearts and let Him in or not. When we open ourselves up to receive the message He is trying to tell us, we will hear it. Otherwise, we close ourselves up to it.

"I know you received that special message because you were searching, and the Holy Spirit was working in you to find it. The others were not prepared to receive it—that's just all there is to it. I understand completely. Sometimes I feel like I'm preaching at a wall between the people and myself. But I keep trying because I know that God is using me to deliver the message of Christ, and I go out there every week believing that there is at least one who will go away with the message and do something with it."

"So you are saying that the Holy Spirit is actually talking to me?"

"Yes. That's exactly what I'm saying. There is no big loud voice, Janine. It is the Spirit himself moving within you, stirring up your soul to get you to turn toward the thing that you are to do. God talks to you this way. He brings you to Himself, and He points you in a direction that will fulfill His purpose in you. It's a marvelous thing, Janine, and God has chosen this time to take you somewhere to do His work through you. Give him the praise and allow him to deliver you."

"What is it that I'm supposed to do?"

"I'm not sure. He isn't talking to me about it."

They both smiled, although Janine was quite uncomfortable at the moment.

"But I would venture to suggest that He wants you to settle down a bit to give Him a chance to let you know."

"Oh dear. I don't know how to do this."

Jim prayed with her, asking God, through Christ, to stay near to Janine, and for the Holy Spirit to keep prodding her until she knew what He wanted. He prayed that Janine would relax her schedule and give herself time to rest and be open to possibilities.

He asked Janine to pray constantly to be near to God and to wait for His instructions.

She felt peculiar. She never, ever found herself in such a place; however, she was also excited because it was truly wonderful and awesome and amazing that God had chosen her for something. She would try to do what Pastor Jim had asked, but how can a person who is so used to being in control simply be still and wait? She had so much to do. She had committed herself to many responsibilities, and she always kept her word and did what she said she would do.

She remembered the "little wind" and how he could not calm himself. The answer would be in the Higher Power, she knew. It was going to take a whole lot of praying for her to change, especially without having the slightest idea what the Lord had in mind for her.

16

The Winds of Change

"Anne, what are you baking up this morning? It sure smells good," Owen said.

"I'm making a lemon pound cake to take in to Laura. I'm going to pick her up this afternoon and go along with her to visit Edward in the hospital. And don't you worry, I'm making one for you too." She smiled, knowing that he would be appreciative. He loved his sweets, and she found pleasure in doing anything for him.

"Well, I'll certainly enjoy that." He smiled in return. "Have you heard anything new about Edward?"

"Laura's encouraged. His heart isn't very strong and he has had a mild stroke, but nothing damaging at this time. I don't know how they will continue to manage the farm, Owen. Laura has taken over a lot of the work, you know, as well as taking care of the house."

"Laura always has been a very strong woman, Anne, but I agree. Changes quickly cause many to have to make major decisions. That's going to be challenging. They have farmed ever since they got married sixty years ago."

They knew the Davidsons very well and were nearly the same age. Laura and Anne enjoyed the homemakers' groups, and both couples participated as 4-H leaders over the years.

Anne sat down at the kitchen table with Owen. "I suppose it's really difficult when you have lived in the same home for so many years. That's one thing different about us, isn't it? We've moved—how many times now?" Anne asked.

"Well, without counting, I'd say five—maybe six. But we've been here for twenty-five years, at least," Owen said.

"Twenty-seven, actually."

"It's the longest we've stayed, but it was the right move. I'm glad we decided upon it. It's been a good retirement home here in the country."

"Yes, it has, and even better now that Alexandra and her family have moved back to the area from Texas. We've been truly blessed, Owen."

"Yes. I wouldn't change a thing."

"Well, maybe we shouldn't become too settled with the way things are," Anne interjected.

"Why not, Anne? What else could we possibly want?" "Oh, I don't mean to suggest that we are lacking anything at all, Owen. I'm just thinking that perhaps we should take a close look at our situation and what the future may hold for us. Will we need to make any changes? I've been thinking a lot about that lately, especially since Edward has taken ill again."

"What are you suggesting?"

"I'm suggesting that we might want to sell this big house and move into a condominium."

"My gracious, Anne! Where did that come from?"

"Just think of it, Owen. We have four bedrooms here, and all on the second floor. We have . . . what? Twelve steps up into the house itself? We park our car out in the garage and have to walk, rain or shine, to the house carrying whatever we have. Look at this kitchen. It's huge—much larger than we need anymore. Our family gatherings are now usually at Alexandra's, due to her insistence. Will we soon be struggling to keep up this property and the house? Heaven knows the years are catching up with us. It would certainly be better to move while we are in good health rather than being forced to make decisions under arduous circumstances."

She could see that Owen was disturbed by her sudden proposal about moving. She was too. She hadn't planned to bring this up just yet.

"Well, I never dreamed you were thinking about this at all. I don't even know what to say," Owen said. "Do you have a place in mind?"

"Actually, I do," Anne said. "You remember the nice place that Helen Stoaks moved into a while back?"

"Yes, of course I remember her selling the farm and moving after Benjamin died. It's very nice. I enjoyed visiting her there."

"It was hard for her, Owen, making so many decisions on her own. Well, anyway, they are constructing another building alongside of the one she moved into. I know what Helen paid for hers, and if the others sell pretty much the same, we can afford to buy one. I'm confident that we could get a decent price for our place here."

She had apparently already put her calculating skills to use.

"Whoa, there. You are really getting ahead of me. I'm not on the same page with you. Let's take our time. All right? You are throwing something at me that I just can't swallow all at once." Owen had decided that he would not discuss it anymore, and Anne knew it.

"I'm sorry, Owen. I didn't mean to jump into all of this today. Let's just drop it for now. Maybe we'll want to talk about it some other time," Anne said.

She knew when she had come to a place with Owen. They had been married for more than half of a century, and perhaps she knew him better than he did himself.

"Maybe," he said. He picked up the book he had been reading earlier, ending the conversation.

ɤɤɤ

Anne and Laura had a very nice visit with Edward. He seemed to be feeling reasonably well and might possibly be going home before Sunday.

Driving up to Laura's home after the visit, Anne asked, "Is there anything I can do for you, Laura?"

"Well, thanks, but you know how the boys are. They are in and out all of the time, seeing to whatever they can do for me. I'm never alone for a very long stretch."

"Yes, I know. You are very fortunate to have both of your sons and their families living within fifteen miles of the homestead, and I know how eager they are to help you. But in case anything comes up, though, and you need something in a hurry, I hope you know that Owen or I will be happy to run over and do anything we can."

"Yes, Anne, I do know that, and it is comforting. Believe me, I'll be fine. Thanks so much for being with me today, and for the pound cake. It is, without a doubt, the best pound cake I have ever eaten. I always hurry to get a piece at our church dinners." "You're welcome. Call us if you need anything. We'll see you on Sunday if not before."

They smiled as they parted, and each was thankful for such a good friend.

Laura entered an empty house. She felt empty herself. What in the world would she ever do without Edward? They were so much a part of one another. They breathed the same air, thought the same thoughts, enjoyed all the same things, and shared a deep love for one another. She walked a little heavier across the kitchen floor, uttering a little prayer that Edward would be able to come home soon.

She saw the note on the kitchen table.

Mother, the cattle have been fed. Someone will be over to see you later on this afternoon with supper in hand. Fred will stop by to see Dad today and bring us up to speed. We'll talk later. Put your feet up for a while. Love, Erica.

She felt comforted with the loving concern of her family. She and Edward worked hard, but they received much in return—much more than they deserved, she thought. She was going to put the cake away, but decided on eating a little sliver and drinking a glass of milk. She sat at the old wooden kitchen table that had been in the family for generations. Ed's Bible was there, as usual, with his class study book. He always began his mornings very early studying the Word.

She traced her finger along the nicks, gashes, carvings, and water rings on the old table and smiled. "*F. D.*" Freddy was in the second grade and had his first penknife. *Ha! He should have known better than to carve his own initials.* The old table could never be replaced with anything else. It had seen the children, served friends, opened up to great gatherings, and had cloths of linens dressing it for very special times. She thought of the bridal reception for Hannah with her grandmother's best Irish linen cloth and roses picked fresh, still dripping with the morning dew. Everything had been so beautiful in soft ivory and pinks.

She found consolation sitting there with her memories, her glass of milk, and Anne's delicious and thoughtful gift.

She was a bit tired, after all. She decided to go sit in Edward's recliner. In moments, she was off to sleep and smiling with sweet recollections and gratitude for God's goodness to herself and to her family.

Anne found Owen outside by the shed gathering up fallen branches. The spring rains had brought down the dead ones, as one expected each year. Owen loved the out of doors, but as he had stiffening arthritis now and didn't move around as well as he thought he should, Anne would have liked it better if he didn't go outside and take any chances of stumbling over something when no one was around. But he had a mind of his own, and she would not attempt to thwart his ability to use it. Considering how many people their age were suffering from dementia, she would be thankful for what they have been given.

"Hello, Owen. Are you enjoying this beautiful afternoon?"

"Hello. Yes, but I've done enough. I'll be coming right in."

"That's fine," she said.

She had prepared a dish before she left the house earlier, and she took it out of the refrigerator and popped it in the oven. She was getting a little hungry, and Owen was always ready to eat.

Owen had come in, washed up, and sat down in the parlor to watch some of the news while supper was being readied.

The afternoon faded into evening, and as was their routine, they went to bed around 9:30 p.m. Nothing more was said concerning the house and the condominium. Neither had felt any need to discuss the subject.

The next morning after breakfast, Anne was picking up the dishes and moving them to the sink when Owen said, "I was thinking a bit about what you said about selling our place here and moving into a condominium."

She truly thought the issue would not likely be brought up again—at least for now—and was taken aback to hear him say such a thing.

"Oh?"

"Um-hum."

That was it? Well, no surprise there. And he got up and moved toward the door leading into the parlor.

She turned to the sink, and he said, "Yep! I think it's a good idea."

She whirled around. *What?* She didn't believe her ears.

He suggested that they go talk to the owners of the new building. He said even now they had to have someone cut the grass here and help care for the property, and he remembered that there were doctors' offices near the condominiums, a barber, and sidewalks to take walks. In addition, many other folks their age lived in the surrounding buildings.

He has given it some thought. This was not as difficult as she had imagined.

They talked about realtors, downsizing, getting rid of furniture, etc.—none of which seemed to bother either one of them. They were both practical people and had always done what they felt was best without looking back. Anne would make a few phone calls.

17

Calling the Realtor

"Good morning! This is Crisscross Realty. How may I help you?"

"Hello. I'd like to inquire about a piece of property you are handling. It's located on McDade Road north of West Hope. The house is brick and sits slightly back from the road. Can you tell me some things about it?"

"Our Mr. Lorey is handling that. I'll connect you."

There was a click on the other end.

"Hello, this is Harold Lorey."

"Mr. Lorey, I'm interested in talking with you about the house on McDade Road outside of West Hope."

"Yes, yes. The Stafford property."

"I'm not sure who owns it, but I have driven by it and would like to see the inside if that would be possible."

"We can arrange that. When would be convenient for you?"

"Well, tomorrow would be fine with me. Perhaps early afternoon. Could I meet you at your office around one o'clock?"

"Of course. I can be here. What is your name?"

"Janine Stephens."

"Fine, Ms. Stephens, I'll see you then."

"That's *Mrs.* Stephens. And thank you."

She hung up the phone, trembling all over. Okay. I did it! Now what? Now I wait for tomorrow. This was just the first step. The others will follow.

ϒϒϒ

This morning, Janine had been startled into awakening. She sat straight up in bed and looked for John who, of course, wasn't there. He was still in Oklahoma.

What's going on? Is there something I'm forgetting to do? What day is it?

She wasn't even sure of that answer. How on earth could she clear her thinking?

She sat on the side of the bed, hardly breathing. She took in a deep breath, held it, and released it—again. *Okay now. Think!*

She couldn't.

I need a cup of coffee, she decided.

She put on her slippers and her robe and headed for the bathroom to wash her face. Afterward, she looked into the mirror and tried to figure out where her mind was. It surely wasn't noticeable to her in any way, shape, or form. She shook her head and went to fix some coffee.

While the coffee was brewing, she put on her jogging suit and walking shoes then drank some coffee and moved herself along, feeling strained to get out and go. She hadn't checked the morning forecast. She only knew that she was ready to go—regardless.

She still had not regained her composure from the startled awakening. She stretched a little, not too much, and headed out on her usual route. She saw nothing of her surroundings; it seemed as though she was moving through a fog.

Lord, are you there? Am I alone? I need you, Lord.

She sensed that she was certainly not alone and began to feel warmth and a calming as she continued to pray. She erased everything from her mind and concentrated on the nearness of God. She knew in her heart that the Holy Spirit was leading her. She began to smile.

I am being touched. I am being led. I am certain of His love.

She was smiling, but there were tears of release and a joy so wonderful, she could hardly bear it.

Thank you, Lord, for loving me. Thank you for wanting to use me. I am yours. Lead me, and I will follow.

She breathed in slowly, and then released her breath slowly. She slowed her walking to a gentler pace, savoring every moment. She knew the presence of the Living Lord, and she did not want to ever be without Him.

Her congregation sang a benediction last Sunday that used the words of St. Patrick of Ireland, which always touched her heart. Today, she was singing it with a complete realization of the importance and impact of their meaning:

> Christ be with me, Christ within me,
> Christ behind me, Christ before me.
>> *Yes, Lord, be with me.*
> Christ beside me, Christ to win me,
>> *You have won me, Lord.*
> Christ to comfort and restore me.
> Christ beneath me, Christ above me,
> Christ in quiet, Christ in danger,
>> *You and You alone, Lord, can do all of this.*
> Christ in hearts of all that love me,
>> *I pray that all of my family will discover the depth of your love.*
> Christ in mouth of friend and stranger.
>> *Your Kingdom come on earth as in heaven.*

She rounded the corner to her home and immediately decided to drive out to the house on McDade Road. She wouldn't go on to Kathy's today. Her destination would be that warmly inviting home that sat there waiting for her.

Without any doubts whatsoever, she picked up her car keys and her purse, poured a cup of coffee into her traveling mug, grabbed the banana she had forgotten earlier, and headed out the door to enter into her future—a future she knew was already planned for her.

Who could be afraid of that?

She was still smiling as she drove into West Hope. "Hello, West Hope. Hello, church on the hill. Hello, country store. Hello, hills and trees and green grasses."

She turned onto McDade Road, and as she drew closer to Bear Track Lane, her heart began to beat faster. She became incredibly anxious and hoped that she would not see anyone from her family today, as she had nothing to say to them and needed to be by herself. She saw the house and the sign that was still posted by the realtor. *Thank goodness!*

She pulled into the driveway and drove down and around the back so that no one would see her car parked there. She did not feel as though she were intruding. After all, she was there for a very good reason. She sat there absorbing and enjoying the surroundings for several minutes and then, without a shred of doubt as to her rights, got out of the car and walked over to the back steps and up to the sliding doors. The curtain was drawn, and she couldn't see a thing inside. It simply didn't matter. She walked back down the steps that led to the backyard, turned, and looking toward the house, felt that she had come home.

Oh, just look at you, so beautiful and hospitable. Do you know who I am?

It was, as she knew it would be. It was right! Without the slightest consideration about details or arrangements, she knew that she would be moving into this house before long. She had no idea why she should be moving or why this was the place for her. She was totally confident that it was in accordance with *The Plan*.

She sat on the back steps for a long time. How blessedly quiet. There are no distractions here.

She thought of the little wind in the devotion and knew that she would be much more likely to realize that calmness in surroundings such as this.

A beautiful cardinal began to sing from the very top of a pine tree. *How can he balance there?* From somewhere in the woods, a song came in response. She was immediately drawn to the prelude of a duet. Soon the two birds were closer together and were singing the same song. These birds didn't seem to be uncomfortable with her presence, and in a little while, other birds began to come closer to the backyard also. *Are those sparrows?* She realized that she really didn't know. She needed a bird book. Then she heard the glorious sound of a robin in the apple tree. The robin's solo voice became the descant to a pleasant and happy chorus unlike any other she had ever heard. *Someday I will add my songs to theirs, and we will praise God together.*

"*Joyful, joyful we adore Thee, God of Glory, Lord of Love.*" The song was in her heart, but she kept it there between herself and the Lord. She would not interfere with the perfection

of the song that was being offered.

Janine returned to the car, immediately called the realtor from her cell phone, and arranged to see the house with him the next day.

She was happy, but a bit of reality struck her as she returned to her house on Alamont Street. She began to assess the situation. First and foremost, how is John going to react to this? Will he think I've lost my mind? Well, I haven't! I'm very clear about this. I'll just have to convince him. That's all there is to it!

There was definitely some shifting to be done with her schedule due to the fact that she would be gone all afternoon tomorrow, and John would be home on Thursday.

I miss him so much. I need to get organized here and plan on a nice dinner for him when he comes home. He'll have so much to tell me, and it looks like I'll have a few things to say myself. Just as she was reaching for the telephone to call John, it rang.

"Hello."

"Hi, honey."

"Well, I was just going to call you. How are things?" "Oh, we're about as busy as we can be with the building, but it is near enough finished now so that Harry and Rhonda can complete the final touches on their own. Nice job, and I enjoyed being able to help. It's been a wonderful experience and a joy to be with the family. We all miss you, though. Really, you'll have to make sure that you come the next time."

"I know it. And I will. I think I am ready to slack off of so much work, John. I want to have time to spend with you now that you aren't an eight-to-six guy. We have a bit of catching up to do."

She could almost feel him smiling on the phone, and she realized that she was serious about her statement.

"Great. Great! I'll tell you, you need to spend more time outdoors. It's invigorating and healthy for our age. I feel stronger, have a tan, and have enjoyed more days in a row than I can remember. Topping it all off, being with the boys was just super. We'll have to find things to do together, Janine, in some good old-fashioned country air. Maybe we can spend some time helping out at Kathy's too."

"I think spending time in the country air is a great idea. We'll just have to talk about that when you get home. There is most likely a perfect solution just waiting to be found. In any event, I can't wait to see you. We have plans to make, you and I."

She could almost feel the hair on the back of her neck standing up, and she tried not to let her voice tremble with the excitement she was feeling. The life that the two of them shared was good—yet predictable. It was obvious to her that they were going to enter into an extraordinary and uplifting chapter, and she was bursting with anticipation.

"Well, I need to get off of the phone, Janine. Harry is expecting an important call from the office. I'll see you around four o'clock on Thursday. Keep an eye on the flight schedule. Who's going to meet the plane?"

"I would love to be there, but I think it will be Greg. I'll stay at home and fuss up for you and have dinner ready. You will be starved. You never get any food on the airplane anymore," Janine said.

"That's fine, honey. You go ahead and fuss up. I like that. I love you. I'll see you soon."

"Okay. Wonderful. I love you too. Give the boys big hugs for me, and give my love to Harry and Rhonda. Bye."

"Bye."

She sat there, nodding her head affirmatively. *The Plan* was shaping up. She didn't need to steer this boat, so she might as well enjoy the ride.

18

Moving On?

Easter was over, and Francine had hoped that another organist/choir director would be located by now. Lawrence's mother, who lived in Florida, wasn't feeling very well, and the place that Lawrence bought down there a few years back had been sitting empty far too long.

"I'll speak to the session again this week, Lawrence. They had very few leads the last time I talked with them. The young woman that we thought would work out was truly not qualified. We *will* take a few weeks in June, no matter what. I feel sure that something good is going to come along soon. Would you like to go on ahead first? I could join you later."

Lawrence could answer that question without even thinking. "I waited all my life to find you, Fran, and I'm sure not going to spend another day without you. It's you and me from now on. Anyway, I believe you are right. I know our prayers will not go unanswered. I'll work a little harder on patience."

"Good afternoon. I'm Janine Stephens here to see Mr. Lorey."

"Yes, Mrs. Stephens. I'll let him know you are here."

Mr. Lorey came out of a back office. Short introductions ensued, and he suggested that he drive them both, which had been her thinking all along.

He was a friendly young man, neat, and full of chitchat. He certainly had the right personality for selling, and she enjoyed the ride with him; however, he was searching for answers without asking, and she caught on easily. She cautiously didn't divulge much of anything personal, and she certainly was not going to have him think that she would be buying a house today.

They didn't go the way of West Hope, which suited her best. She was too personally involved with that endearing community to be sharing a drive through it with a stranger.

They pulled into the driveway and walked to the front door. He led her to the entry and went to turn on the lights in the living room. Janine had firmly decided that if the room would not accommodate her baby grand piano, she would remove all thoughts of this house from her mind. She entered the room with the possibility that the answers to her future might not be found here.

She was astonished to find an incredibly large room—probably big enough for two baby grands! *Okay, Lord. Okay. That's a pretty impressive response to my little threat. You must have been quite amused with my little dance there.* She caught her breath and treaded on with the discovery process very carefully, uncomfortably realizing that she had been putting herself in charge of His Plan.

She didn't bother measuring anything for furniture placement. No point in that.

It was a well-kept ranch-type home with all the living area on one floor. It certainly wasn't formal like her present home, but she didn't expect it to be. It did have the oddest-looking color of green on the walls. *John is a terrific painter, so that won't be a problem.* The house was eighteen years old, so the kitchen could use some upgrading, but the best part of the kitchen was the sliding doors to the upper deck.

We could put a nice table and chairs out there and sit with our coffee and morning paper in the summer, and there would be no one to see us if we decided to go out in our pajamas. We wouldn't hurry because we would not be on a time schedule. That's what retired people were supposed to do. She began to sing the song in her head: *"Summertime, and the livin' is easy—"*

"Mrs. Stephens . . . ? Mrs. Stephens."

"Oh, sorry. I was just thinking of something."

"Would you like to go outside and look around?"

"No, I don't think I need to." She wouldn't tell him she had already done that yesterday.

"Would you like to go downstairs now?"

"Sure."

The property was listed as having a finished basement. He led her down and waited for her. He was smiling inwardly, awaiting her response.

She stopped before getting to the bottom step. The stairway was open, and she could see everything. *Good heavens!* She had not considered that the downstairs would be "finished" in such a fashion. She had envisioned a one-level house with a "basement."

"It's my understanding that the original builder wanted to have his parents move into the house, and so he designed a separate 'apartment' so to speak."

It was finished with especially fine wood paneling, and it was carpeted. The entire downstairs was one large open space with at least three sofas, chairs, tables, etc. *What possibilities it had!* He took her across, and she discovered a full bathroom and—of all things—a complete kitchen. A vastly *large* kitchen! She was bowled over.

"My goodness! I can't believe this." There were two ovens and a built-in range. Nothing fancy; it was more like an old-fashioned country kitchen. A table was in the center, and if it had extra boards, it could probably open up to seat a dozen people.

This would be great for cooking up outdoor picnic foods, and it could all be carried outside through those sliding doors. She was stunned and drifted off away from Mr. Lorey to the outside doors and stood there thinking of the boys. She thought of what fun it would be for them to visit, play down here, and run in and out. *We should put up a basketball net out there and hang an old-fashioned swing onto that big old tree.*

She was totally won over at that point and had to control herself not to say something stupid like "I'll buy it."

Instead, she said she thought she should get on home, talk to her husband tomorrow who was coming in from out of town, and then call Mr. Lorey in a couple of days. He had already told her the asking price, and she thought it fair before she ever saw the downstairs. Who would have imagined?

Why had this house not been sold before now? She thought of the day she had seen the "For Sale" sign and of the other events leading up to this day, and she had the answer to the question.

19

Coming Home

There he is! Janine was beside herself with the prospect of having her husband back home. Dinner was ready, and she had been literally pacing the floor for the past ten minutes. She saw John get out of the SUV and say something to Greg as he smilingly headed straight for the front door. They met on the portal and greeted one another in an embrace that meant so much to them both. It was sweet of Greg to wait a few moments before getting out of the vehicle to unload John's luggage. After a kiss or two, John turned to carry a few things, as well. Greg graciously excused himself to go home to his family. John and Janine went on inside and kept smiling and looking at one another.

There were questions about the days spent apart—mostly from Janine, as she wanted to be brought up to date on everything about their little family in Oklahoma. John had many little stories to tell, and he touched on a few as they sat down to dinner.

With the kitchen cleaned up and the luggage moved out of the living room, they sat down with their evening coffee and talked for hours.

When Janine moved into the subject of her experiences with the devotion she had given and the lack of interest by her women friends, she was on a mission to tell it all to John. He was so interested that they talked past midnight. He nearly sat on the edge of his seat as she told of her walk this week and her encounter with the Holy Spirit.

"That is absolutely awesome. I've heard of people being filled and moved by the Holy Spirit, and I do know for a fact that he exists because I have felt him lead my life. I would love to have *that* kind of personal connection, Janine."

"It is totally awesome, John, as you said. And another thing . . . It gave me strong assurance that there is something I am being called to do. I have to tell you, I don't know what it is just yet, but do you remember telling me when you lost your job that Reverend Jim said God has plans for us?"

"Yes, I do, and I have never been worried about it either. I know that everything is going to work out for the best."

"Well, I didn't have the confidence then, but I sure do now!"

"Good. Let's just relax and go into the future together, Janine. It's going to be very special for us. I know it."

"I have more to tell you, John. I hope you won't think I've totally lost my mind when I do."

She knew that John would not judge her too quickly, so she told him everything about the house on Bear Track Lane.

She began with the sign in the yard and ended with her visit there with Mr. Lorey yesterday. She kept looking at John the entire time, trying to figure out what he was thinking. He just let her talk.

"Okay," he said.

"Okay what?"

"Okay . . . I guess we'd better call Mr. Lorey and arrange a time for us to go back to the house to see it together."

She jumped up, plopped onto his lap, threw her arms around him, and said, "You are the best husband in the whole wide world. Thank you. Thank you. So you don't think I'm crazy?"

"Well, I wouldn't go that far," he said.

"John!"

He laughed and hugged her tightly. "You know what? I think I like you this way—suddenly unpredictable. Yep! I like it. I'll tell you another thing. This has to have been planned out by a higher authority because you never, on your own, would have even thought of it."

"You're right. I'll call Mr. Lorey in the morning. Now let's get ready for bed. I've been waiting to cuddle up to my warm bed buddy long enough."

ᵞᵞᵞ

There were no hitches in anything that occurred the next day. Mr. Lorey was free to show them the house. They both decided it would be a good move, and legalities were put into motion. John and Janine had not discussed putting their house up for sale, but naturally, Mr. Lorey was Johnny-on-the-spot in that regard. He suggested that he stop by and take a look at the house on Alamont Street soon, and perhaps he could work with them for an expedient sale and move.

John and Janine felt like two newlyweds starting out all over. It was exciting and exhilarating, and all the potential problems, such as Janine's job at the church, did not trouble them at all. They just knew it would all work out.

Janine even typed out the words from Romans 8:29, which she had learned years ago from her grandmother. These words assumed newfound meaning to her today: *"And we know that in all things God works for the good of those who love him who have been called according to his purpose."*

She printed it out on colored paper with a nice border and magnetized it onto her refrigerator. "God is all goodness, and is so very good to me. Grandmother, you were absolutely right."

20

Julia Remembers

Julia Gillanders lived alone in a house built around the turn of the century in the very small borough of West Hope, which was nestled in rolling hills between larger communities. The town had no need or desire to grow into anything other than what it was. Folks were born here and pretty much stayed. Everyone knew everyone else, and that's the way they liked it. She pulled herself to her feet and looked outside. As she expected, Prudence Eldrich was out sweeping the cobblestone sidewalk in front of her house across the street.

Honestly! She's going to wear out those old stones. How they've lasted this long, I'll never know . . . especially hers. I'll bet she's swept them ten thousand times! Emily thinks it's her excuse to go outside so she can watch everything that goes on. Maybe so.

The cobblestone sidewalks that have been in West Hope for two centuries were "quaint" to some and "stumbling stones" to others. The question of what to do about them has come before the borough council many times, but probably won't be resolved. "Change" is not likely to win any votes here.

Julia lived right on the main—and only—road through the town. Friends used to stop by on a warm summer's day to sit awhile, but many of those friends are now gone or are too old to be venturing out much alone.

Well, that's the price to pay for living so long, I suppose. Whatever!

It began to rain, and there seemed to be a chill in the air; so she took her old sweater from the hall tree, put it on, and wished she had something to think about besides being lonely.

She looked over at her half-finished crocheted doily. She had made so many of them, given most away, and was not much interested in them anymore. Her eyesight was poor, and it was quite a strain to read the directions—more trouble than it was worth!

Her optometrist had told her she needed to have her cataracts removed. She was planning to do that soon, but it wasn't easy to work out the transportation in and out of Innesport. Iola had told her that the Senior Citizen van would come to West Hope to drive her into the city. They scheduled those trips from early morning, dropped people off where they needed to go, and picked them up around five or six o'clock to take them back. That would be a long day, but she had decided—rather than ask a friend to drive her, she would call the senior organization and see what she could work out. That, of course, all had to be scheduled with the date of the procedure.

Life is more and more complicated every day, and it's not much fun either!

She sat down and, as usual, began thinking of happier times. Lately, she had decided that she would choose her topic of recollection. Yesterday, she spent time reminiscing about the games she would play with her brothers and sister. Her parents had named her Juliska, a nice Hungarian name. They usually called her that at home, but when she began to associate with outsiders, her parents told everyone her name was Julia. They did not want her to be discriminated against, although her mother would use her given name when she was speaking to her in loving terms.

She thought of the neighborhood and of the other immigrant families. They were from different countries but came together as children—learning to speak the new language, playing tag and hide-and-seek, and gathering up ball games. Every one of them was similarly poor and didn't even know it. She smiled. She had had a wonderful childhood running, laughing, and playing outside all day.

Today, she would think about her children. She missed them now that they were grown, married, and living away from her. She didn't blame them for seeking a better life, but it would be nice to have them nearer where they could be together at least for a birthday, or even a weekend here and there. But she wouldn't think about that. Today, she was going to think of them living here in this house, making noise, chasing each other, celebrating holidays and such.

Let's see. I'll start with Charlie's first day of school . . .

Somewhere along the way, she dozed off in her chair. She often did that. When she awakened, she realized that it was after noon. She should go fix something for lunch so that she could take her arthritis medication and her blood-pressure pill.

She pushed herself up, noticed that it was still raining, walked to the kitchen, and opened a can of soup.

Well, at least tomorrow is Sunday. I can go to Sunday school, talk with the others, and catch up on how everyone is. We'll probably go to lunch afterwards. I'm not going to have soup. Seems like that's all I eat anymore. I think I'll order a piece of chicken and some mashed potatoes and maybe join Bea in a piece of pie. Yes, that's what I'll do. Look at me. I'm shrinking away to nothing. I used to be thirty pounds heavier and was taller. I didn't like the weight before, but now I think I could use some. Oh well. That's the way it goes, I guess. You get old, and what's left?

The soup was hot. She sat down alone at her table listening to the rain, sipping the soup, and putting in the hours of another long day.

21

Puddles and Obstacles

Iola MacCowan looked at the rain and decided not to go for her walk today. She usually drove over to the park and walked around and around where there was little to no traffic. She would just exercise to the tapes she bought.

The Pittsburgh Pirates baseball game would be rained out, so she would not watch television. That was one thing she did enjoy now. She used to teach music, but her hearing was weakening, and the hearing aids made things sound horrible. Sometimes they would squeal and pierce her brain. She decided they were hardly worth it. She knew she was missing out on most of what was being said around her, but until she found a doctor who could get her the right hearing aids, she would have to live with what she had. There weren't many people left to talk with, anyway.

She walked to the nearby post office every morning. She would greet the people present with a "good morning," and she could comprehend their return response. She avoided staying any longer than politely necessary. She did not want to engage in conversations that would force her to strain to hear the other person. She simply greeted then moved quickly on.

Her special telephone amplified the sound coming in, so she could have a telephone conversation. Otherwise, she simply turned the volume up on the TV or radio and that was that.

Harriet and she were good friends, and sometimes they did things together. Harriet was one of the few who would, without being irritated, repeat things to her when necessary.

Iola would spend today planning the menu for the Women's Association spring dinner at her home. She had hosted that event for the past few years and enjoyed it. It was several weeks away, but she was a planner and liked everything organized.

This time, she would use her good china and fresh flowers on the dining room table. Maybe she'd make use of the tablecloth that her husband's Aunt Polly had left to her. It was hand-embroidered with delicate little flowers. She'd match the fresh flower to that.

I'd better start writing things down and checking them off. I don't know if the tablecloth needs to be freshly laundered or not, so I'll check on that first thing.

Iola came to West Hope following her marriage to Lester. He was a third-generation McCowan, and he could not fathom living anywhere else.

They had a good life together here with their children until his unfortunate death, leaving Iola alone to fend for herself and her children. Everyone thought she had managed better than most anyone else could. She taught public school, Sunday school, and made very sure that her children were brought up "right." The community embraced the young widow and was eager to look after the children when necessary. She often wondered if she could have done as well in any other place.

She wished today that she was doing the things she used to do. She felt that she still had wisdom, strength, and vitality to be of service, but most people didn't notice. She was not thought of when it came to calling upon someone for advice or leadership roles. She, like most women her age, was looked upon as a person to respect—but used up and rarely included. So she would read, go to church, and once in a while offer a suggestion that no one took into consideration.

Oh well. Lord knows I've tried. I guess I've had my day.

22

Rachael Ventures Out

Well, I might as well face it. The rain is not going to stop. I'm going to go to town, anyway. I need to pick up my prescriptions, and I want to get to the craft store so that I can start on those frames.

Rachael Wimber gathered up her coat, purse, and color swatches. She picked up her umbrella from the entry hall and zipped out the front door. The car was parked beside the house, and by the time she got there, she was damp from the waist down. The rain seemed to be blowing sideways.

She sat in the car until it warmed up some, ran the windshield wipers and the defroster, and headed down the drive to the road. Albert had scraped the road just before Easter and added some gravel, which was now well packed, so there wasn't a slippage problem. She eased her way down and was on her way.

She was thinking of the grocery list she had left behind. She racked her brain to remember everything she meant to pick up for the soup she was planning to make the next day. She enjoyed making every kind of soup and usually kept some on hand for

Albert to have at lunchtime. One of her primary pleasures was to prepare a nice warm lunch for him. He lived nearby with his family and worked his land and Rachael's.

She would be making fresh chicken noodle soup this time.

She turned out of the borough and crept along slowly eastward through shrouded visibility. There were very few vehicles on the road. *I probably shouldn't be here, either. I'll be careful . . . I'll be fine. I should be back home in less than two hours.*

The disgruntled driver of a delivery truck entered West Hope from the west. He lit another cigarette and squinted through the windshield as he was attempting to hurry along. *I hate havin' deliveries on days like this. And I hate even worse workin' on Saturdays. I should be with the guys in Lou's Bar havin' a few beers and watchin' some sports on ESPN. If I don't waste too much time, I can still stop in at Lou's and catch up.*

The driver was wearing the same black T-shirt he had slept in the night before. He needed a shave, but didn't care. Since the divorce, he was free as a bird—just the way he liked it.

He went through West Hope well over the speed limit and gained even more speed on the open road. He didn't see any cars, so he pressed down on the accelerator and decided this was a good place to make up some time.

Driving past The Orchard Restaurant, he looked into his rearview mirror and noticed a car had pulled out but had turned the other way. Good. *He won't be followin' me.*

He rounded a bend in the road and suddenly came upon a very slow-moving car. *What the . . . ! I could have rammed right into the back of that car.*

He slowed down but stayed closely behind the car. He began flashing his lights and determined that the driver was a little old lady.

Well, just my luck! "Hey, lady! Move it or get it off the road!" he said aloud. He flashed his lights some more. She didn't seem to notice, maintaining her turtle crawl.

"Git off the road, you old biddie! You got no business bein' out if ya can't drive!"

Now he was practically on her bumper. *Maybe I'll just push her off the road.*

The lights caught Rachael's attention, and the truck seemed hazardously close. She knew the man was irritated with her slowness. She sped up a bit, but it didn't seem to satisfy the driver of the truck. She would pull off when she could. In the meantime, she'd give him a little more speed. As she moved forward from him and looked in the rearview mirror, she struck a huge puddle of water in the road. The tires she had meant to replace a month ago were worn to the point of no traction. She hydroplaned and struck the edge of the road, throwing the car out of control. It landed in a ditch on its side.

The truck driver uttered every word he had learned on the streets, slammed on his brakes, and came to an immediate stop.

"Now look what you've done! And it's all your own fault! People like you need to know that you're too old to drive.

You're a hazard to the road and a hindrance to people like me who have a job to do and a real purpose in life."

He put his Budweiser ball cap on and got out of the truck. The rain was still hammering down, and he was soaked instantly as he walked over to the car. The wheels were still spinning. He tried to open the door, but it was locked. The woman was either dead or unconscious, and the motor was still running.

His instincts guided him to get something to pry the door open and turn off the engine before the car burst into flames.

He ran through the rain to his truck and grabbed a small crowbar just as a car came from the other direction. The driver of the car rolled down his car window and asked what happened.

The man answered, "It's an old woman locked in there. I'm going to try to pry the door open and turn off that engine. Do you have a phone?"

"Yes. I'll call 911."

The truck driver, imitating a noble and blameless person, said thanks and ran to the car. He pried open the door without having to break in through the window and turned off the engine.

He did not want to touch the bloody woman who was slumped strangely sideways. She might be dead. She looked dead for sure. Without remorse or an iota of guilt, he conjured up the courage to touch her neck—and felt a pulse. He jerked backward as the sensation sent a weird shock throughout his body, and he came close to vomiting. He had to get away from the sickening scene.

The man from the car ran toward the scene and asked if he could do anything, and the valiant "savior of the road" quickly collected his thoughts and said it would be best if they just waited for the emergency car. He walked over to the gathering crowd, enhancing his role and enlarging his ego by answering questions and asking everyone to try to stay calm. He was reveling in being the hero of the day. In fact, he wanted to tell all about it to anyone who would listen.

When the police arrived and questioned him, no one could dispute anything he had to say . . . except the unconscious old lady. But by now he was so convinced of the magnitude of himself that he was positive she would be grateful for all his help. *She should be grateful! I'm sick and tired of havin' to put up with stupid people on the roads!*

He repeated to the questioning officer that the lady was driving much too fast for the road conditions.

"I blinked my lights at 'er hopin' she'd slow down, but she didn't pay no attention. It's sad to see the fix she's got 'erself in."

The officer wrote down the necessary information on the truck driver and told him he could get on his way. "Just be available for further questioning if necessary, Mr. Tredway," he said.

"Of course. I sure will. If I can be of any help at all, please let me know."

"Thank you. You've already been a substantial help in this tragic situation. The emergency car is on its way."

The truck driver, proud of the way he had smooth-talked his way out of trouble, got back into his truck and gingerly pulled away. He hoped he would never see any of those people again in his life.

ϓϓϓ

Marvin and Marcia Severight, owners of the apple orchard and friends of Rachael, drove up to the accident. They rushed out of their car, recognizing the car in the accident as Rachael's. Marcia spoke with the police officer and found that her condition was grave. She was granted permission to see the victim, but even with her nurse's training, she was helpless to do anything. Thankfully, the E-car and medical team arrived a few minutes later. Rachael remained unconscious as she was prepped and moved into the medical van.

Marvin held Marcia's hand as they stood in the rain listening to the siren fading into the distance, taking their friend to city hospital. She told the officers she would contact family members. They went to Albert's first, who left immediately for the hospital. Marcia assured him that she would call his sister Celeste, the pastor, and others.

ϓϓϓ

When they arrived at the pastor's home, Pastor Dan met them on the porch.

"Come in. Come in. It's nasty out there."

Water rapidly dripped from their bodies. They hesitated at the invitation, but upon Dan's insistence, they did go in as far as the kitchen. His wife Patricia was there as well. Few pleasantries were exchanged as it was obvious that the Severights were upset. Chairs were pulled from the table, and Pat immediately put on a pot of coffee.

"What is it?"

"It's Rachael Wimbler. She's been in a terrible automobile accident. We were there minutes after it happened. She was still unconscious when the EMTs were moving her. The ambulance took her to city hospital."

"Oh dear. I'll go right away. Why don't you stay and have a cup of coffee with Pat? You could make a phone call from here and start the prayer chain going if you want to."

Pat handed Marcia the telephone and the phone book as she nodded her head. Before leaving, Pastor Daniel too their hands and led them in prayer. Then he picked up his jacket, his Bible, and the keys to the car.

Marcia called Rachael's daughter, Celeste, who didn't stay on the telephone any longer than necessary. She would immediately arrange to leave the office as soon as possible. Continuing with her calling, her heart pounding, and silently praying, she was appreciative of the warm cup of coffee. So was Marvin. Pat was a beautiful and gracious lady, and everyone loved her as much as they loved their precious pastor. They could count on her for anything at any time.

They quickly left to go home and get into some dry clothes; however, Marcia would not be able to sit still. She would have to freshen up and get to the hospital as soon as she could. She was number one on the phone list. She was also "A-number one" as a caring individual.

23

A Praying People

The community of faith was on its knees when Marcia finally changed into dry clothes and headed out for the hospital. She assured Marvin time and time again that she would be careful, and she was. She found Celeste and Albert in the emergency waiting room.

Albert was on his feet. "Marcia, thanks for coming. Pastor Dan is here also. He stepped out for a moment to see if he can get some information. We've heard nothing so far."

"I had to come," she said.

Celeste was so worried that she hardly noticed Marcia enter until Marcia sat down beside her and took her hand.

"Oh, Marcia, I'm so worried."

"I know. I know. Let's not jump to conclusions. There are many prayers being lifted up for Rachael. She's in the Lord's hands, and He will carry her through this."

"Family of Mrs. Wimbler?" the doctor asked.

Albert stood. "Yes, Doctor. I'm her son Albert, and this is my sister Celeste. Our pastor is here with us. This is Mrs. Severight, a friend."

"Mrs. Wimbler is conscious but highly sedated. We are still checking her over for injuries. We're getting pretty good vitals, but she has broken bones—primarily in her feet, and we suspect some internal injuries. We want to have her transported to Allegheny Hospital as soon as possible."

"Is she stable enough to move?" asked Albert.

"She is, and we believe that her injuries warrant it."

Albert looked at the others, and it seemed to be the consensus that the move was the thing to do. Who could question the doctor in this instance?

"Doctor, is she going to be all right?" asked Celeste.

"I really cannot answer that right now, I'm sorry to say. She will receive the best of care, I do know that. If you are a praying people, it wouldn't hurt."

"There are a lot of people praying for Rachael," said Reverend Dan.

"I encourage you all to keep it up," said the doctor.

"Believe me, we will," said Marcia.

"I'll call Tavia and let her know that I'm going to drive on up to Pittsburgh. Celeste, do you want to come with me?" asked Albert.

"I think I'll wait here for Erica. She's on her way, and I know she'll want to go too. We'll be right along."

"Albert, I would like to go with you, if that's okay with you," said Pastor Dan.

"Thanks very much. I'd appreciate it."

Albert went to call his wife, and Marcia said she'd wait there for Celeste's daughter to arrive.

Pastor Dan encouraged Albert to let him drive, and Albert agreed.

"Can we see Mother?" asked Celeste.

"You and your brother and the pastor can come in for just a minute."

The three left the room with the doctor. When they returned, Celeste and Albert were both in tears. Marcia understood and embraced them both.

"They are going to prepare her for the move. It's still raining, so they've decided to use an emergency car instead of the helicopter. The doctor said that they have a great team of trained personnel to go along with her, and we are satisfied that it is going to be a safe ride for Mom. They will get there in no time, so we'll be leaving right away," Albert said.

Just then, Erica came and was briefed by her mother, Celeste. The four left quickly in two separate cars.

Standing alone in the empty waiting room, Marcia began to tremble. The tears could not be held back any longer. She sat down and did what she did best. She called upon the Lord for His comfort, strength, and assurance. The Lord answered her prayers, and she was finally able to call Marvin. She relayed to him information about Rachael and said she'd be coming home right away. Marvin said he had fixed a little something for them to eat.

What a dear he is, she thought. *I probably will be hungry. I don't know. I don't feel much of anything right now but concern for Rachael.*

She did welcome the smell of food when she entered the house and the best hug in the whole world. She stayed with the hug for quite some time.

They sat down together, ate the food, talked, and both settled into an exhausted sleep.

24

Morning Has Broken

Julia, Francine, Paula, and the other members of the church awoke on Sunday morning to a beautiful day of pastels as the sun's rays peered through soft clouds of pinks and purples. Each welcomed the end of the storm and prayed that the feeling of hope brought forth by the clearing weather was the signal of answered prayers.

Few stayed at home that day, for it was surely a day meant for gathering together and praying.

Pastor Dan had arrived at home only an hour before morning prayers commenced. Albert went on home to change clothes, and the others stayed behind to be near Rachael.

Every person who saw the pastor asked the question: "Is Rachael all right?"

He answered, "As well as can be at this point. Keep praying."

The ladies were early to Sunday school. They immediately started talking about the accident and things they might do to be of help to the family. They would not be driving into Pittsburgh to visit, but there would be other things to do. They were all very concerned.

"Rachael has had so many problems," said Julia.

"She sure has. How she ever came through that heart attack is beyond me," said Bea.

"Well, Rachael always said that the church prayed her well. You remember how she used to say that?" Julia said.

"I remember. And then there was the time she had to have surgery on her stomach. She was laid up for quite a long time then," Anne said. "But she bounced back, and she will again. We must not give up hope."

"No, we won't. We will pray her well again. Rachael always said she doesn't know why she is still here. Well, I know why! God answers our prayers, that's why. And he knows that she is such a shining light in our world here. We just can't do without her," said Bea.

They all agreed. Little was done about the lesson that morning, but just being there with one another meant everything. They had prayer and signed the card that Harriet had for them. Their Sunday-school teacher always came prepared.

They dismissed, feeling a little better just having been together. They always did.

ϒϒϒ

"Great God, we worship You in praise and thanksgiving, and we seek Your blessings upon all who are gathered here and upon those who could not come today." Pastor Dan continued his prayer, which was lengthy and heartfelt, as he called upon the Lord to lead the church and the flock to do His will in the Kingdom.

The church joined in his sincerity, and when Pastor Dan implored the Lord for Rachael's recovery, they were uttering the plea deep within their souls. They knew that God had pulled Rachael through incredibly serious illnesses, and they believed their prayers would be answered once again.

The scripture was read:

> *I lift up mine eyes unto the hills, from whence cometh my help?*
>
> *My help cometh from the Lord, which made heaven and earth . . .*
>
> *The Lord is thy keeper: the Lord is thy shade upon thy right hand . . .*
>
> *The Lord shall preserve thy going out and thy coming in from this time forth, and even for evermore.*

It was from Psalm 121, which was a major theme for this church on a hill in West Hope, and it was resonating in every ear and in every heart with promise through faith today.

The sermon did not fall on deaf ears that morning. Pastor Dan must have revised his sermon during the night, because it spoke directly to the situation that existed within the Body of Christ that morning. It was spiritually uplifting and comforting to all. The congregation knew from "whence their help would come." Who could ask for anything more?

ᵧᵧᵧ

There were people in church that morning who rarely attended. A few of Rachael's friends were there because they felt drawn to be with the gathering on the hill.

Hayden and Elda Carter exited the church and walked down the hill toward their home in the center of the borough. They owned the general store and lived in the house beside the store. They were friends with Rachael and many of the other church members. They usually attended the African Methodist Episcopal Church (AME) located in a nearby community, but today was just different. They wanted to be with Rachael's friends and join with them in prayer, and they were glad that they had been there.

ᵧᵧᵧ

Many of the locals enjoyed gathering at the Carters' on weekday mornings—not always to shop but surely to chat, pick up the morning paper, or sometimes share a story or seek advice. Ms. Elda always had a big pot of coffee brewing for the neighbors, and sometimes on Wednesdays and Saturdays, there were cinnamon rolls and hot breads to purchase. The aroma of fresh-baking bread in the small community was something local family members would remember when they moved away, and they would tell others who could only dream of such a wonderful thing.

One had to be up early to take home a fresh-baked loaf of Ms. Elda's bread. She liked to bake, and no one knew what she might enjoy baking at any time—whether it be rye, raisin, cheese, or the most excellent plain white in the country. It didn't matter! If she baked it, they would buy it, for they knew it would be the best.

ᵞᵞᵞ

"That was nice," Elda said.

"Yessiree! Reverend Daniel is a good man and certainly is in touch with the Lord. His sermon and prayers were just what we all needed to hear. I'm sure glad we went there today."

"I am too. Tomorrow, I'm going to bake up something for the family. I hope they will be able to come home to rest. These will be difficult days for Albert and Celeste and the children."

"That's good, Elda. You always think of the perfect thing to do."

"Speaking of food, I'd best get busy with today's meal. Leanne and Tommy will be coming in soon. She sure seems to like that boy! I do too."

"Yessiree! He's just fine. You said you put a pork roast in the oven this morning, didn't you?"

"Well, that's what Leanne asked for, so that's what we'll have."

They were home, which was a very large old house in the Victorian fashion, beautifully maintained and very impressive to all that passed. Hayden enjoyed his carpentering skills, and he had made some mighty fine improvements on the old structure.

And of course, Elda had a God-given talent for transforming any room, any porch—anything at all—into something beautiful.

"I'll go change into something else, Elda. Let me know when you are ready for me to help you peel potatoes and set the table."

"I will, Hayden. I'm going to put on my apron and check the roast first."

"Mmm-mmm! I can smell it! What time are we eating?"

"Around one thirty, so we'd better keep moving."

"No trouble for me. I'm hungry—and even hungrier smelling that meat."

25

Decisions, Decisions

The Monday morning newspaper arrived, and many read the article about Saturday's accident, including Greg Lang. Kathy was almost ready to leave for school with the girls when Greg uttered, "Oh, of course!"

"Of course what?" asked Kathy.

"Old Virgil has done it again."

"Virgil? What's he done now?"

"Well, says here that he was the first on the scene of a road accident and that he probably saved the victim's life."

"That's good, isn't it? Why are you so disturbed over that?"

"You know that former brother-in-law of mine has never cared about helping anyone. The only one he cares about is himself. He has pulled the wool over everyone's eyes and painted himself as a fine individual once again."

"Now, Greg. We haven't seen him for quite some time. Maybe he's changed."

"He hasn't changed. He'll never change. I wouldn't be surprised if he was the one who caused the accident. He is the slickest talker I've known, and that slick talker has nearly ruined the lives of my sister and their children."

"What's the paper say?"

"It says that a woman was travelling too fast in the rain, and her car slid off of the road and turned over. Her condition is critical, and she was moved to Allegheny Hospital. Let's see. Virgil came upon the scene, ran to her car, pried open the door, and turned off the engine. The car could have ignited otherwise. Poor old Virgil. There he was in the pouring rain, sacrificing himself to save a perfect stranger.

"I'm sorry, Kathy, but I know that miserable, worthless human being too well to believe this story. I don't know how he does it, but somehow he does. Just seeing his name in print is going to ruin my day."

"I know how you feel, Greg. He almost destroyed your sister's life. But she's doing better these days now that he's out of the picture. Try not to think about him anymore."

He folded up the newspaper and said he would do that, but after Kathy and the girls left, he had to read it one more time.

I hope Amy doesn't see the paper today. She needs to just forget that louse. He picked up his keys and left for work.

ΥΥΥ

Janine hung up the telephone and went outside to find John. He was in the garage.

"Hi, honey," she said. "What are you doing?"

"I'm trying to decide what I should take along to the new house. Everything, I suppose. I may actually find use for some of these tools out there, especially the trimmers and such. Something on your mind?" he asked.

"Are you kidding? I have so much on my mind, I can hardly sort it all out. But I want to tell you that Mr. Lorey just called, and he would like to drop by tomorrow to go through our house, if it's okay with us. I told him I'd call him back. What do you think?"

"Fine with me. I sure don't want to put out a sign of my own and go through all the worry of trying to show the house, search the courthouse records—all the things that our Mr. Lorey could do for us. So if you want to, just go ahead and have him come over. Maybe he can give us some indication of what kind of price we might get for this house."

"Right. Okay, I'll call him. I'm going in to talk with Pastor Jim today about my job there at Center Church. What do you think I should say?"

"I thought you decided that you could continue with the work there, Janine. Have you changed your mind?"

"I don't know. At first, I thought I'd be able to commute back and forth, and I still think I can do that, but should I? That's the question of the day."

"Well, do you have to decide now?"

"No. Not really. I'll just let Jim know that we are moving and about how happy we are. When he hears of the circumstances, he will be overjoyed for us, I know."

"Sounds good. I'll be busy out here for a while. Go ahead and do what you need to do. I'll see you later."

"Okay . . . John?"

"Yes?"

"Are you still sure that we are doing the right thing?"

"Absolutely!" he said.

Janine grinned from ear to ear. "Me too!" she said.

She gave John an air kiss because he was pretty greasy-looking and went on her way.

ϒϒϒ

"Hi, Connie. Isn't this a beautiful day?" said Janine.

"It most certainly is. We've had quite enough rain. I'm ready for sunshine and flowers myself."

"Well, that's just what you're going to get. Enjoy. Is Pastor Jim in?"

"He's in his office. I think he's expecting you. Just a minute, I'll buzz him."

Janine looked around at the familiar surroundings. There were pictures on the wall out in the hallway of past ministers, many of whom she had known and loved. This church meant a lot to her.

"Janine, you can go on in."

"Thanks, Connie."

She had been through this door many times. She and Pastor Jim met often to discuss the worship services and her role as music leader.

"Good morning!" said Janine.

"Good morning to you. Come, sit down."

"I appreciate you seeing me today. I know this is the day you will be meeting with the ministerial group, so I won't keep you long."

"That's fine, Janine. I have lots of time. What's up?"

She wanted to be brief, but her story about her encounter with the Holy Spirit and ultimately deciding to move into another house couldn't be shortened. As she was describing the morning she had awakened with so many questions and, subsequently, the walk, Jim was on the edge of his seat, as excited as she was.

"And, Jim, after walking through that house, it felt so right. I just knew. I had no doubts whatsoever. It was so wonderful, and knowing that the Lord Himself was leading me gave me such a marvelous feeling of being blessed. Oh, I can't put it into the right words. I'm sure, though, that you realize what I'm trying to tell you. You were the one who told me that the Holy Spirit was drawing me into something when I talked with you before."

"Janine, I am so happy for you! This is truly the work of the Lord. I believe that many are blessed, but few comprehend it. It is a positive advantage that you recognize this."

"Well, thanks to you! You opened up my mind to an awareness of what was happening to me. Thanks so much, Jim. I sure wouldn't want to have missed this for the world. We'll be moving soon, more than likely. I think I'm supposed to be doing something over in the West Hope area, but I sure don't know what."

"Don't worry about a thing. If it's the Lord's will—and it sure sounds like it—it will all work out."

"Thank you, Jim. I'm going to stay with Center Church until I know that I should leave here. Maybe I won't have to, but if so, you will have lots of notice. Okay?"

"Whatever will be will be, Janine. Let's not even try crossing that bridge right now."

They talked about John and her family and the prospects for a different kind of life for her. Neither knew just what that was going to be. It didn't matter to either of them. She was ready. Janine felt fortified and excited when she left the office. She was thankful that she could talk with Pastor Jim and her beloved John. Who else would understand?

Well, I'd better wait and see where all of this ends up. God certainly has a plan, but knowing His timing, it could take years.

26

Two by Two

Mr. Lorey came the next day. With the house's condition and potential marketability, he felt that it would sell quickly.

"You'll need to have the house appraised. I could recommend someone to do that," Mr. Lorey said.

The Stephens agreed, and from then on, it was unbelievable how everything seemed to fall into place.

First, the purchase of the house on McDade Road moved right along. The price was agreeable, the owner was happy, and papers were being drawn up. Secondly, Mr. Lorey was handling everything that needed to be done concerning the sale of the Stephens' house. There would be no problems as far as anyone could see, except for the immediate problem of having to tell the children!

"John, this is going to be the hard part. They will be certain that their parents have lost their minds."

"I know. Have you thought about how to approach this?"

"Every time I think about it, I push it aside and think of something else. I thought of going to Kathy's for lunch and talking with her alone. She might be happy to have us move nearer to her. That may be presumptuous, though. In this day and age, families do live apart, and they adjust and possibly like it better."

"Maybe," John said.

They both sat there, staring into space for what seemed like a long time.

"How about if we set up a tour of the house with Mr. Lorey and have Kathy and Deb both go with us?" John suggested.

"Hmm, I don't know . . . John, I truly hate having to face all of this. If we could just go ahead without having to stir up the family, wouldn't that be great?"

"Well, that's not going to happen. We have a family, and a close one at that. We don't want to hold back from one another. We always told the kids that, didn't we?"

"Yes, that's true. You're right. If they see the house, they just might understand. Of course, I don't expect them to feel the same as we do. Nevertheless, let's try it that way. Things are moving so quickly, I guess we shouldn't put it off," said Janine.

ϓϓϓ

"Deb, did Mother call you?"

"Yes. She invited me to your house for lunch on Saturday. I said I could come. Is that okay with you?"

"Yes. I'm happy about that. What else did Mom say?"

"Nothing much, really. Is something wrong?"

"I don't know." Kathy hesitated. "She seemed to have something on her mind, but didn't want to tell me."

"Well, she didn't tell me, either."

"It's probably my imagination. I'll see you around eleven thirty on Saturday. Okay?"

"I'll be there," said Deborah.

27

Apple-Blossom Time

Marcia was keeping busy waiting for Marvin to come in from inspecting the apple trees. During the spring, he was always motivated to walk all over his beloved orchard and enjoy the thrill of new life. The winter pruning was completed just in time for the spring season, and the workers had done an excellent job of it. Some of his friends were retiring from their lifelong careers. Not Marvin! He loved what he was doing and would continue it as long as the good Lord allowed.

He came in through the kitchen door, all smiles. Marcia was occupied with something.

"Did you enjoy yourself?" Marcia asked.

"I sure did. Things are looking pretty good. I saw a few blossoms—our favorite time of the year. And guess what?"

"What?"

"I'm still singin' the song."

"Did you sing it today when you were walking?" Marcia asked.

"Yes, I did." He started singing: *"I'll be with you in apple-blossom time."*

She joined in, adding her alto harmony. They had been singing that song for forty-some years now and had never tired of it.

They continued into conversation about the trees and their plans for a new grove this year while Marcia set some lunch out on the kitchen table.

"We'll be getting busy again from now until Christmas, but I'm not complaining. I married you for the apples."

He grinned. She always said that.

"Remember at Easter when the boys were talking about coming again for the summer? They love being here and working the orchard. The cycle continues, doesn't it?" Marvin said.

"Looks that way," she said.

"When Carl came home from college and decided to stay with the orchard, we were so happy. And now his son Jason will be going off to college this year. Do you think he'll come back and want to build a house here like his dad did?"

"Jason has worked here since he was eight or nine years old. He'll be back," she said.

"I hope you're right."

"In the meantime, Jason will still be here for a while before he goes off to college. Luke and Joshua will be coming from New Jersey, as they said, and staying here with us. I do love having them around and cooking for them. It's going to be a good year."

"It is. With Carl and Jason and Luke and Joshua, we'll be right on top of things. How about Amanda? She's bound and determined to get right in there with them."

"She's only eleven, Marvin. She thinks she's smart enough and strong enough too. She may be right, but I say give it another year. Carl thinks she'll be very happy working in the barn selling later in the season. It will be a good start for her." "It's such a blessing seeing the children following 'in the footsteps,' so to speak. Dad would be thrilled with the progress we've made over the years. It's not the big business it could be, Marcia, but I think we agree that it's the right size for all of us today. Who knows what the future holds for our children?

Anyway, that's for them to decide. In the meantime, let's be thankful for what we have."

"I agree."

They finished dinner discussing the children, apples, and hope for the days ahead.

"Oh, I almost forgot! I have some good news," Marcia said. "Rachael seems to be improving. She has an awfully long way to go before she will be up and about, but she *is* showing signs of improving. She has so many broken bones in her feet, though, that the doctors wonder if she will ever walk again. Poor Rachael. That is just so sad. But I know she will overcome anything. If she can't walk, she'll do what she can as she sits. She will never throw in the towel."

"When is she coming back from Allegheny?"

"There's no word on that right now. Thankfully, she had minimal internal injuries, but she will have surgeries on her feet, leg, and I don't know what else. Maybe we can go see her sometime soon."

"Sure. When do you want to go?"

"Well, maybe Friday. How's that sound?" "Sounds fine. Let's plan on it."

28

From Scene to Shining Scene

Marcia and Marvin Severight drove through the countryside that was more than familiar to the two of them. They smiled when they saw a few apple blossoms on the trees near the farmhouses. The forsythia and the daffodils had given way to yellow and red tulips. Purple azaleas were in bloom, which were always the first of such bushes to show their color, and the softly-beautiful yellow irises were slow dancing in the gentle breeze.

"Whenever I see the irises, I think of Bea Roberts. She has them lining her driveway. She said she would be thinning them this year and will give us some if we want them. Have you ever smelled the yellow iris, Marvin?"

"I'm not sure."

"You would remember if you did. It has a subtle spice fragrance. There is nothing quite like it. I remember how surprised I was. It was not like a flower, and yet just as pleasurable. The fragrance would be suitable for a man's cologne, I believe. I'm not sure if all irises have the same scent as the yellow. Anyway, we'll have some of our own, thanks to Bea, and we can enjoy them over and over again. They bloom every year by May first, she said—and in some years, again before the end of summer. Maybe we'll stop by Bea's this week and just take a sniff. I want to be there when you do."

"Isn't that nice of her? How old is she, Marcia?"

"I think she's eighty-two or eighty-three."

"Wow! She sure gets along well for that age. I see her cutting her grass and sometimes even on her knees digging around her flowers. She has some unusual flowers and some for every season, it seems."

"Well, she's a trooper and determined to not let anything get her down. She also seems to have a terrific wit. I'd like to know her a little better, but I haven't had much opportunity."

Soon they were on the interstate and moving right along. Marcia was glad that Marvin was driving into Pittsburgh because she was not all that comfortable driving alongside, in front of, or behind aggressive drivers. She enjoyed her country roads and would rarely, if ever, venture into Pittsburgh alone. She did her shopping in Innesport most of the time. There were a couple of malls there, lots of specialty stores, and anything she would want or need. She had been driving those roads since before the malls had ever been built, and she had been acclimated to it all in a gradual way.

They came to the hill known as Mount Washington, which completely shielded from view that which was behind it. The only indication that they were nearing the city was the increase in the traffic that was now merging into two lanes. They entered the long, lighted tunnel, and she knew that as soon as they exited, they would see a most spectacular sight. She, like many others, anticipated the moment with excitement. The amazing "Golden Triangle" of Pittsburgh with its tall, shiny buildings would suddenly be presented to the traveler on the other side of the hill. Today, with the sun shining brilliantly on the glistening buildings and the bridges, she was once again greatly impressed.

Two rivers converged at the point of the triangle to form the beautiful Ohio. As they crossed the Monongahela River, they could see many bridges filled with cars moving toward the city over the busy waterways augmenting the energy of the city.

They had planned to enter Pittsburgh around 10:00 a.m. to avoid the rush-hour traffic, and it worked out well. In no time they were at the hospital, taking the elevator to the floor where Rachael could be found.

They quietly peeked around the door—she might be sleeping.

"Hello!" Rachael said.

"Rachael! We thought you might be resting," Marcia said.

"Are you kidding? No one rests in a hospital. Come in. Come in. It's nice to see familiar faces."

She was in bed with her legs wrapped and resting on pillows. "They did a little repair work on my right leg the other day.

Thankfully, it wasn't a really bad break, and I shouldn't have much trouble with it."

"That's so good to hear, Rachael. How are you feeling?" "I don't know. I can't get up at all. I have to keep my feet elevated. Apparently that's where the trouble is. I don't know just when we'll find out exactly what is broken and what can or cannot be fixed. I am worn out trying to scoot myself into some kind of comfortable position right now."

"Oh dear," Marcia said.

Marvin sat down in a chair by the window.

Rachael told Marcia that she was totally unaware of anything about the accident, which Marcia said was a blessing. Marcia went on to tell Rachael that she and Marvin had arrived on the scene shortly after the accident occurred, and it had been a very scary situation.

Rachael said, "I suppose I should be glad to be alive. Once again, Marcia, I cannot understand why the good Lord wants me here. I've had many opportunities to leave this world, and it seemed like it would be a good thing if it happened, and yet He doesn't take me."

"Well, that's not for us to question, is it?"

"I think it is! And I do! If there is something He wants me to do here, He sure is not giving me much to do it with. I do question it! I truly think it would be better if I just went on. I actually haven't been of much use for years."

"Rachael! I can't believe my ears. Please. Think of the wonderful works you have done, even after the last time you had that stomach surgery. There is definitely a lot you can and will do with your talent and creativity. You'll figure it all out with God's help."

"Marcia, I don't want to sound ungrateful, and I'm trying to accept the hand that has been dealt to me, but this time, I wonder."

Marcia was feeling so sorry for Rachael who was always the one to lift everyone else's spirits. She was cheerful by nature and always looked at tasks as challenges to be conquered.

Rachael loved to read, so Marcia had brought her a couple of books. One book was a funny but true story about the history of the MacKintosh Clan, of which Marvin was a descendant. She had picked it up from her coffee table this morning in order to hopefully give Rachael a good laugh about the carryings-on of those Scots.

The other was a day-by-day devotional, which she hoped would help her through these difficult days.

They stayed until the physical therapist came to see her. Rachael had said that they would probably keep her there at Allegheny until they had her on her feet—or at least had done all they could for her. It could possibly be a few weeks.

They said their good-byes and reluctantly left her. She did give Marcia and Marvin one of her wonderful smiles, which they knew was meant to lift their spirits. That was Rachael for you. She would be the one. It was her calling. Even as she lay completely incapacitated, she would want to help someone else. Marcia was touched by her beautiful gesture, and she knew why God had not taken her yet.

We must all try to help her along. She will need our support.

29

Opening Doors

They drove out McDade Road and resisted the temptation to stop at the "new" house. They couldn't get in, anyway. Mr. Lorey would have to be there to open the doors. Janine was nervous. John gave no indication whatsoever of anything.

As they turned into Bear Track Lane, she said, "John, we certainly have been giving the girls things to think about lately, haven't we? I can't remember when there was a time like this when we felt the need to talk everything over with them. We've been going to *them* with discussions of changes instead of them coming to *us* as always."

"We're not just talking . . . we're sharing. That's what families do."

"I know, but it is *different* somehow."

"The tides flow in, and the tides flow out," he said.

"What's that supposed to mean?"

"Okay. How about this? What goes around comes around."

She looked at him glaringly. Where was his sensitivity? "John, John, John. Give me some encouragement here. I'm a wreck."

"I *am* giving you encouragement," he said.

"No you're not. You are throwing adages or proverbs at me. I need for you to say something like, 'Janine, dear, everything's going to be just fine.'"

"Ha!" He actually laughed and thought that was funny. She, however, did not!

"John!"

"Okay, Janine. Look. You are getting yourself all shook up before you have a reason to. Let's just flow with the tide and see where it's going first."

"That's easy for you to say, 'Mr. Solid-as-a-Rock.' I'm feeling more like squishy mud."

"Well, you'd better get out of the sinkhole. We're here."

She took in several deep breaths in an attempt to collect herself, straightened her body, brushed her skirt, and got out of the car. As usual, there was Prince. It felt especially good today to give him hugs, and he returned the warm gestures with lots of sloppy, slurpy licks. Janine smiled.

Granddaughters Karen and Meghan were on the porch, waving.

"Hi, Grandma! Hi, Granddad!"

"Hi, girls!" they responded.

Uh, oh! They didn't consider that the girls would be home. *Why not? It's Saturday, of course! What could they expect?* Janine was wondering if this day could possibly turn out all right.

"John. John . . . wait! Don't go in yet. Listen! We can't take the little girls along. We need to have Deb and Kathy alone, don't you think?"

"Well, all we have to do is tell Deborah and Kathy that we want to take them somewhere and that we won't be long. The girls are old enough to leave behind, if that's what you want to do."

Janine took in another deep breath. "Okay. That's what we'll do." They hurried on up the path to the house.

"Hey! You're here. Come on into the kitchen. How about some coffee?" asked Kathy.

"Mmm. Perfect!" responded Janine as she hugged her daughter.

Deborah was already in the kitchen, and when her parents arrived, she hugged them both. They proceeded to sit down at the kitchen table.

Small talk ensued, as always, when *real* questions are not being asked.

"It's a beautiful day, isn't it?" asked Deborah.

"It sure is," answered Janine. *Is it really? I hadn't noticed.*

"Here's your coffee," said Kathy.

"Wonderful!" said John. He had decided not to open up the conversation about the house. He did not want Janine to feel caught off guard, so he left it up to her to initiate the topic.

"So . . . what have you two been up to?" asked Kathy. "Oh, not much. Things have eased up since Easter, and it's good to have your dad home. He's been cleaning up the garage."

"Spring cleaning, I suppose," Deborah said.

"Sort of," he responded.

Janine drank her coffee.

Kathy went over to the refrigerator and opened the door. John and Janine could not see her behind the open door. She used her hidden circumstance to glare at Deborah as if to say, "Now what?"

Deborah shrugged. "We have everything ready for lunch," she said. "What do you say? Are you hungry?"

"Yes. Let's go ahead and eat. Are the girls joining us?" Janine asked.

"No, they are going to walk Prince over the hill behind us to the stables there. Meghan can hardly stay away from there. They had made arrangements with the neighbors to be there today, and I gave them an early lunch. I'm sorry to disappoint you. I know you'd love to have them join us, but we'll do this again real soon."

John responded quickly, "Hey! That's fine. They'll have fun."

Well, there you are! That's settled, and I had nothing to do with it. Janine looked at John, who was snickering, as only she would detect.

Ha! *Look at him. He is always so confident. It's a good thing because, at this moment, I could use a little confidence myself.*

Just then, the girls came in dressed for the hike and eager to go.

"Mom, we're ready," they said.

"That's fine, girls. I've already told Grandma and Granddad that you would be leaving. Be very careful, and be home by two o'clock as we planned."

"Okay. We'll see you later," Karen said to all of them as she turned to leave.

"Have fun," John said.

They were gone, lickety-split. They were talking excitedly as they went out the backdoor with Prince bounding along.

"Well, here we are. Let's say grace and enjoy," said Kathy. "Dad, would you?"

"Lord, be our guest at this table. We thank You for your many blessings. Bless this family, this home, and the food we are about to partake. In the name of our Lord, Jesus, we pray. Amen."

"Ummm, mmm. This soup is delicious. Did you make it, Kathy?"

"Well, it wouldn't be that good if I had made it. Greg made it for us, of course."

It was a delicious bowl of Manhattan clam chowder. Janine preferred the red to the creamy New England style. She didn't think she would be able to eat, but the soup changed all that.

"John, just taste this bread. My goodness, it's delicious.

Did Greg bake this?"

"I got the bread this morning over in West Hope. I had to be early to get it. You would not believe the rush to get to the little store there on Saturdays. That's the day that the owner's wife bakes bread—Saturday and Wednesday. But they tell me you can't be sure what kind of breads she might bake. It doesn't matter. Everything she bakes is delicious. I'm really glad, though, that she made this whole wheat for today. Isn't it really great?"

"Well, how about that? I've wanted to go into that little store. What else do they have?" asked Janine.

"Everything! You wouldn't believe it. It's so nice and clean, and if we need anything, we can usually find it there instead of driving on into town."

"Well, well," said Janine. She and John looked at each other. They each knew what the other was thinking.

"The other day, I needed a light bulb and bought it there . . . and get this! Once, I just had to have yellow thread. I thought 'No way would they have that.' But they did. They have what's necessary in the grocery line, even a deli, and hand-dipped ice cream cones!"

"Well, that's really something. I never dreamed . . ." said Janine.

"I've found lots of surprises around here," said Kathy.

"We have too," said John.

"What does that mean?" asked Deborah.

"Well, you'll see," he said.

Janine was sitting there wishing he had not said that. The girls were looking at them with questioning eyes, and she did not know how to proceed.

"Okay now. What's all of this about?" asked Kathy.

"Really! Why don't we get on with it? Is everything okay?" Deb asked.

"Everything's fine." John decided that he needed to take the bull by the horns and immediately get this show on the road. "I'll tell you what. Come with us. We have something to show you. Can the girls get in the house if they get back before we do?"

"Yes, they can, but where are we going? How long will we be?"

"Oh, not very far. We will most likely be back before two o'clock. Is everyone finished eating? John asked.

"We are now!" said Deb.

"I'll turn off the stove and wrap the bread. I'll only be a minute," said Kathy. She hustled, wondering what in the world they were going to do. Deborah helped her as Janine went into the powder room to freshen up and collect herself.

Soon they were all leaving in John's car. Deborah and Kathy sat in the second seat. Kathy reached over and grabbed Deb's hand and squeezed it so hard it hurt. They were sure of nothing! They just kept looking at one another, full of questions.

In no time, they were pulling into someone's driveway. *What's this?*

There was another car there, and a nice-looking young man got out of it. John and Janine told the girls to come on, and they too got out of the car.

"Hello, Mr. Lorey. I hope we didn't keep you waiting," said John.

"No, no. I just got here myself. How are you?"

"We're fine. Please meet our daughters, Deborah and Kathy. This is Mr. Lorey, a sales representative for Crisscross Realty," said John.

They shook his hand. *Wait a minute! Sales representative? Why?* They were both thinking the same thoughts.

"It's very nice to meet you. I've heard so much about you both and your families."

Well, that's just lovely! I've heard absolutely nothing abut you! thought Deborah.

Mr. Lorey? What's he doing here, anyway? What are Mother and Dad doing? thought Kathy.

Mr. Lorey said, "Let's go on inside."

Inside?

"Yes, let's do. But if you don't mind, Mr. Lorey, you go ahead. We want to speak to Kathy and Deborah for a minute," said John.

Janine was thinking, *Okay, John. You just do that!*

Mr. Lorey went on inside of the house that had the "Sale Pending" sign on it, and the girls turned to John waiting for something—anything!

"Now then, here is what we want you to see. The house."

"The house? This house? What about the house?" they asked.

"Well, here's the thing . . . We are buying it."

Oh boy! Now he's done it! Janine was so nervous she could not look at the girls. Good grief! *What are they thinking? What can they be thinking? They don't have enough information to assimilate the situation.*

Janine finally cleared her head and faced up to the situation.

"Girls, listen! I know this sounds crazy. But it's the truth, and we need to tell you all about it."

"Oh my gosh! This is totally a shock. I don't even know what to say," said Kathy.

"I don't either, but I guess we don't have to say anything, really. We'd better just let Mom and Dad do the talking."

"And we will. Come on, girls, let's do go inside. Okay?" Janine said.

"Just a minute, please," Kathy said with her hand on her mother's sleeve. "Are you going to move here? Are you going to sell our house in Innesport? I'm sorry, but I just don't understand."

"Yes, that's right," said John.

"Holy cow! What brought this on?" asked Kathy.

John smiled. "Holy it is!"

"What?" the girls chorused.

"It is such a long and wonderful story. Your mother can tell you all about it . . . then you'll understand, I'm sure. But in the meantime, just know that we have decided to buy this house." He led them to the front door. Janine let the girls go, and she followed.

"Father in heaven, be with us. Please help John and me to find the right words here. Thank you, Lord. Amen."

"Mom, are you coming?" Deborah asked.

"Yes, of course."

ϒϒϒ

Mr. Lorey said he would be downstairs and excused himself. John and the girls waited in the entryway for Janine, and then they went on into the living room. There was a picture window letting in light from the outside, which was helpful because the lamps weren't bright enough to light the room. *Older people tend to be conservative on wattage.*

The sofa was well worn with scarves on the back that couldn't hide the orange and faded yellow flowers on a brown background. The girls looked at it and could hardly see anything else. Janine noticed the sofa for the first time. It hadn't been of any concern to her. It would soon be gone.

"This is certainly a very large room," said Deborah. They all agreed in one way or another.

"I was so happy when I saw that my piano would fit in here. I was thinking beforehand that if the piano didn't fit, I probably wasn't meant to live here," said Janine.

"Well, it's certainly not a problem, is it?" Kathy interjected. She was so shocked over the situation that she didn't know what to say at this point and couldn't imagine her mother's baby grand piano any place other than their home on Alamont Street.

Janine and John were discussing which would be best—see the rest of the house or hear the explanation of their decision. It was hard to decide.

Finally, John said, "Girls, really, the house is fine. It's not the house that matters. There is something more important about all of this, so I think we need to let your mother tell you all about it. Let's sit down. Okay?"

They looked at Janine, and she began, "Well, for a while now, I had a peculiar sensation that there was something I was supposed to do, and since I didn't have the slightest idea what that could be, I began to be nervous and questioning. Due to a few somewhat unusual occurrences, I went to speak to Pastor

Jim about it. He advised me to wait and listen because he thought that God was trying to tell me something, and that I would no doubt be finding out soon."

"Really . . . That's interesting," Deborah said.

"It is. It's also wonderful and amazing. One of those unusual circumstances occurred at a meeting of the Women's Association at our house. You remember, Kathy, right after Easter, I went home to prepare to entertain and to work on devotion for that?"

"Yes, I do."

"Well, while I was doing my best to figure out that devotion . . ." She went on to describe the story of the little wind, the ladies' non-reaction, her disturbance, etc. "So I certainly understood when Pastor Jim told me that there have been many times that he felt he had a message that needed to be brought forth and sensed that no one heard it at all. His explanation was that their hearts have to be ready to *receive* the message.

"I'm sure that I myself have heard hundreds of messages and didn't grasp the intended meaning. I've even read the same scripture many times over without coming to a true understanding. Then a day would come when suddenly, out of the blue, I would get it! Did that ever happen to you?"

"Yes, it wasn't too long ago, either," Kathy said. "It was at one of our Bible study group meetings. We were looking at a scripture that I had practically memorized, and there was a message for me that day that I had not received before . . . I know what you mean."

"I thought the little story was wonderful, Mom. And you know what? It seems to me that it was meant for *you* more than anyone else. You do stress yourself out a lot by trying to do too much for too long. It puts you in a tizzy like that little wind," said Deb.

"I know. I know. I'm working on it, but it's going to take a lot to settle me down. Anyway, I'm not finished yet. Wait until you hear the rest of the story."

Janine told them of her encounter with the Holy Spirit.

They were completely mesmerized.

She went into details about how she had been overly interested in this house from the beginning and how very strange that seemed to her. When she felt compelled to come back the day of her encounter, there was positively no holding her back.

Janine felt better being fully upfront with the girls, although the recollections and explanations were beginning to take a toll on her. John could tell she was exhausted recalling it all, and he jumped in to tell them about the visit to the house by both of them and of their unqualified decision to move.

"We didn't really have a choice, girls. I believe, as much as your mother does, that we both belong here at this time. You know, God has a purpose for all of us. Sometimes that purpose puts us in a different place. We are both excited to learn what that might be, and we want to get to it as soon as we can. We hope you will be okay with all of this."

"My goodness! How could we not? It's wonderful. What can I do to help?" asked Deborah.

"I feel the same. And the bonus is—you'll be closer to me! The girls will love that too. It's going to be just great."

Both girls jumped up and hugged their parents, offering their support.

After tears of joy from all four, they decided that they definitely should look through the house, after all.

They saw a lot of things that needed to be done, which Janine hadn't bothered to acknowledge before. She assumed that she had turned a blind eye to all that.

"No problem. I'll have lots of time to fix things up, paint, and so forth," said John.

"Hey! Don't forget about us! We'll help too. Now what about our home in the city?"

"Well, it hasn't been sold yet, but we'll get ready to move out, anyway. We've settled on a price for this house, and the final papers will be signed soon. We sure could use a hand in the moving," John said.

"I have to admit that it's going to be hard for me to see my past disappear in front of my eyes. I have all the memories of my childhood in the rooms of our home there," Deb said.

"I know, honey, and I understand too. But life goes on, just as it did for you and Robert. We need to let go of the past and, with faith, walk into the future. It will be fine. You'll always have those memories, just as you have now," said Janine. "I truly never expected to move from our house there on Alamont Street. This is so sudden, and we will all have to adjust, that's for sure."

"Well, ladies, have we seen enough? We should let Mr. Lorey get home. He's been so patient with us today, and it's almost two o'clock. The girls will be getting home," John said.

"Yes, we'd better go." Kathy turned to Janine, "Mother, it's a lot different living out here in rural America. Set your mind for it. I hope you will love it as much as I do."

"You know, I have been telling a lot of people, even before all of this happened, that it is so great out here in the rolling green hills. I think God has been setting my mind for it for quite some time. I'm not saying it will be a piece of cake, but I'm ready."

ϓϓϓ

"Deb, what do you really think?" Their parents had gone home, and Kathy was eager to speak to Deborah alone.

"Mother and Dad feel the importance of this. I can't deny that. It's certainly virtuous and upright, Kathy. I do think Mother may have a hard time adjusting to this completely different way of life. She is so used to the social life in Innesport. However, you moved out here, and you love it," Deborah said.

"You just can't compare my move with this move of Mother's! The quiet life suits me so much. But, Deb, look at the life she has had! 'Mrs. Society!' And she's always enjoyed it," Kathy said.

"People can change. That's what God's expecting from her, and He'll help her, so let's not worry ourselves about it." Deborah seemed perfectly comfortable with what may lie ahead.

Still considering the obstacles, Kathy replied, "But what if after she sells and moves, she sees the house with all of its flaws? Then will she step back and lose her balance?"

"It's not the house, Kathy. Even Dad said that."

Kathy took in a deep breath, realizing that she was focusing on the wrong thing. Her mother had been handpicked for something special, and she had responded. They should emphatically rejoice with her, give their support, and wait to see what's going to happen.

"You're right. I'm worrying. What kind of trust is that?" "Sometimes our love and concern get in the way," Deb said. "She's one solid lady."

"She is."

30

"Click"

"You're going to do what?" Bea asked.

Every member of the Sunday-school class was waiting for the answer, even though they heard Anne the first time. This would give them time to think of what to say in response.

"Owen and I are going to sell the house and move into the Birchwood Condominium Village."

"When did you decide this?" Iola asked.

"Oh, we've been talking about it. There comes a time."

"Those are really nice apartments," Julia said. "I looked at them once, but just couldn't make up my mind to move. It's such a big job getting rid of everything. I don't think I have the energy to do it, anyway."

"Me either," said Bea. "Of course, Anne, you have Alexandra and her family to help."

"Oh, we'll be fine. We'll basically give the children and my nieces and nephews whatever they want, sell the rest, get a moving van to do the moving, and that will be that."

Anne was the most practical person in the world. Nothing disturbed her. She made decisions, figured it all out, and it was done. The gals all admired Anne for her courage and assertion whatever the situation. There wasn't one person there who would want to pick up and pack up and do what she was doing.

Jenny McMurray had been Julia's closest friend for many years, but she had moved out of the borough a while back. Her family was gone now, and it was too much for her to maintain the large family home and property. She sold it and never looked back. She had been very well satisfied with her new and beautiful apartment on the other side of Innesport. The only problem was that she rarely drove back to see anyone anymore and only occasionally got to church. The class was very pleased that she came today.

"Anne, I'm happy for you," said Jenny. "There is no need for you to work your fingers to the bone in that big house. I think it is very smart of you to decide to do this while you have your senses and capabilities, and also while you still have Owen to go with you."

As Julia listened to her dear friend Jenny, she was beginning to see the inevitable. Now, not only Jenny would be absent from them much of the time, but it appeared that Anne might be also.

A stillness settled over the room as the dear friends all sensed an end approaching.

"But, Jenny, we hardly ever see you anymore," said Julia.

"I know, and I'm sorry about that, but you know my back is not good anymore, and the long drive is almost too much for me."

"Anne, if you move out to Birchwood, will you and Owen get back to church?" Laura asked.

"Oh yes. We'll be coming here for church. At least, that is our plan."

Laura had appreciated so very much Anne's friendship throughout the years, and especially during her husband's recent hospitalization. Anne and Owen and Laura and Edward had enjoyed many experiences together. Like Julia, Laura felt a bit of uneasiness hearing these words from Anne.

Julia interjected her thoughts: "I worry that our class is going to fade away."

Iola said she did too. The class had been together for many, many years and once even included their husbands before a men's class was formed. Now they were down to just a little more than a handful of women.

"We only have each other, it seems," said Bea. "Every last one of us needs to keep trying really, really hard to stay together. Look at us. One, two, three, four, five, six. Adele is away, and most of the time, Jenny can't come. Francine does try to bring Alice, but not as much anymore. Anne . . . please don't desert us."

"I won't."

The certainty of separations known and unknown actually slowed the cadence of their breathing and filled their hearts with a weighty heaviness. After a time, Iola spoke up. "We should try to get more people in this class."

"Now just who would you get?" asked Bea.

"I don't know. Rachael, maybe." Iola was usually the hopeful one.

"Rachael is flat on her back!"

"I know. Has anyone heard how she has been this week?" Iola asked.

"She had surgery on her leg and got along well with that. It wasn't too serious, but she is still in Allegheny and can't stand on her injured feet," Harriet, the teacher, said.

"Oh my. I don't know. It's hard to imagine Rachael not getting better because she always has. We can't stop praying for her," said Bea.

"I wish we could go see her," Julia said.

Everyone nodded in agreement, but no one really could volunteer to drive anyone else into the busy city of Pittsburgh.

Coincidentally, Marcia peeked into the room. She was on her way to her class with her husband but wanted to stop in and report on Rachael.

"We were just saying that we wish we could go see her!" Julia said.

"I'm sure she would love to see you too. She should be moved back this way sometime soon. She seems depressed."

"No! Not Rachael!" said Jenny.

"Yes, she really does. She is not the same spirited and cheerful person we're used to. She definitely needs encouragement. Hey! I have an idea! My daughter Barbara has that wonderful new three-seat vehicle, and I'll bet she would be happy to drive us up to see Rachael. I'll ask her if you'd like for me to."

"That would be great. When?" Julia asked.

"Let me think . . . How about Wednesday?"

"I don't have anything else to do." "Neither do I."

"Monday, Tuesday, Wednesday—any day's fine with me." "Me too!"

"I get my hair done on Friday. That's it. But I'm sure I could change it," Iola said.

"Let's say Wednesday. Can you be ready by nine o'clock in the morning? Marvin and I find that if we get to Pittsburgh around ten o'clock or so, we miss a lot of the morning traffic."

They all could be ready. Actually, if the truth were known, most would no doubt be ready long before that. They didn't get to do special things much anymore.

"See me after church this morning, and in the meantime, I'll check with Barbara and let you know." Marcia scurried out to get to her class.

"If we're going, I'll meet you at your house, Iola," said Harriet. "Anne, how about you? Can you get away?"

"I'm sure I can. Owen can visit with Alexandra, so as not to have to be home alone. I'll just drive him over there and also come to Iola's. Is that okay with you?"

They were excitedly making plans. It would be fun riding together to Pittsburgh—an adventure.

Bea said, "Can we take her something? We probably shouldn't take food in . . . I know what! How about one of those helium-filled balloons? Or better yet, a bunch of them. Wouldn't she brighten up if we each walked in carrying a colorful balloon?"

Anne smiled. *Leave it to Bea. She would always be the one to find just the right thing.*

Iola said, "Let's not get the cart before the horse here. We don't even know for sure if we're going."

"Well, just in case. Anyway, we'll know before this day is out. Let's decide what we'll do just in case," Bea said.

"Where can we get the balloons?" Julia asked.

"Over at Super Buys. It's on the way. If we leave ten minutes early, it will all work out great." Bea had the answer. They all liked it.

They were smiling and chattering as they left the classroom to attend the service. Harriett realized that they did not get to the lesson, and she was a stickler for seeing that they did not get off track. *Well, Lord knows we need a little diversion once in a while. I'll cover two lessons next week.*

ϓϓϓ

One has to wonder if any of the ladies heard the message that morning. If Pastor Dan had one especially for them, he might want to preach it again on another Sunday.

At the conclusion of the worship service, they gathered together in a cluster at the back of the sanctuary, waiting for Marcia to come to them. She did so right away, with Barbara at her side. They were smiling—a good sign.

The ladies waited and waited there. Opal Harrington had stopped Marcia in the aisle. *Uhhgghh! Anyone but Opal. She's impossible to get away from.*

Church members walked by, and some spoke to the ladies briefly. The church was emptying, and there was Opal, still going on and on . . . Finally! Marcia was free! She and Barbara headed quickly to the back.

"Well, ladies, we're on! Wednesday it is."

They discussed the pickup schedule. Laura would be staying home with Edward, and Jenny said the drive would be too difficult for her, and the day would be too long for Alice. The others were thrilled, and Bea was sure that Adele would be coming with them. They asked about stopping for balloons, and Marcia and Barbara smiled and agreed that was a great idea. They would do the pickup a bit earlier. And one more thing—they would stop for lunch on the way back home!

No better words could have been spoken.

༡༡༡

They all went into the store. Each wanted to pick out her balloon herself. It was a sight to behold! Six elderly ladies, all smiles, were scampering through the store to the checkout counter with balloons designed to cheer. Well, they cheered, all right!

"Look at those ladies!"

"I wonder where they are going with those balloons."

"Well, aren't they having a good time?"

"Look! Have you ever?"

They came outside, bouncing along buoyantly as though the balloons were lifting their feet. Julia—who was never presumptuous or first in line but much more likely to be waiting to see what others were doing—was in front. *I have never done anything so silly-looking or frivolous in my life! I like it.*

They grouped together. *Click.* One balloon was a big smiley face, which represented accurately the inner feelings of the bearers. Bea's idea had been a good one. Without warning or expectations, their gesture of kindness turned upon them and anointed them with gladness.

With difficulty, they managed to get into the van. The crippling pains of arthritis and stiffening hips had been somewhat of a problem when they were picked up earlier. Now, with the balloons, it took a little more figuring out; but they moved past the pains and stiffness, helping one another and laughing themselves right into their seats.

Marcia realized that her suggestion was proving to be as important to the ladies as it would be for Rachael.

Now, with the balloons bobbing up and down and left to right, they were faced with what to do with them as Barbara couldn't see through the back. The ladies would have to hold them down somehow. It was just too funny! They finally found that they could tie the strings around their legs or purses, and they rode all the way to Pittsburgh pretty much nursing balloons on their laps. They didn't care. It was a great day.

Barbara wanted to go in with Marcia alone and be prepared to take a picture that would be a keepsake for each of them for years to come. When the ladies stepped off the elevator, people stopped to look, smile, and enjoy the spectacle of it all.

Rachael was surprised to see Marcia again so soon, and she was pleased that her daughter-in-law came also. Rachael seemed about the same and said that she would have another surgery when she was strong enough. If only she could get up! She couldn't even sit and was still on her back with both feet elevated.

"How am I supposed to get stronger just laying here?"

Marcia excused herself for a moment to tell the others to come into the room. They inched their way toward the door. Marcia went on in. Barbara focused her camera, and there they were—six happy, smiling ladies wanting to share their happiness with Rachael. And they did! *Click.* Rachael almost came out of the bed. *Click.* She was overjoyed just to see them. *Click.* But she would never forget the balloons, the bright colors—*click*—and the joy of that moment. If ever a heart could be lightened, a spirit lifted, and a smile given, that was the time. *Click.*

They talked and laughed. Marcia got teary-eyed. So did Barbara. Giving to another was always rewarded greatly in return.

Marcia thought of the framed scripture given to her when she graduated into nursing:

> *Give, and it will be given to you.*
> *A good measure, pressed down, shaken together*
> *and running over,*
> *Will be poured into your lap.*
> *For the measure you use, it will be measured to you.*
>
> Luke 6:38

It's more than true! I'm the happiest one here today, Marcia told herself.

Barbara thought, *Look at these dear friends! I'm just so happy that I could bring them together like this. I'm the happiest one here today.*

Each of the ladies were thinking, *How wonderful to be here with Rachael and see that great big beautiful smile of hers. She makes me so happy!*

Rachael was praying. *Thank you, Lord, for giving me these wonderful friends who can always put a smile on my face. It sure feels good to smile and mean it.*

31

They Come and They Go

Marcia was calling. "Bea, can I bring Marvin by for a few minutes so that he can see and smell the beautiful yellow irises?"

"My goodness, yes! You didn't have to ask to do that. When are you coming?"

"We're coming by there in about ten minutes, I'd say. I described the fragrance of them to Marvin, but it's like trying to tell someone how chocolate tastes."

"No sense in that. Bring him over. I'll be here!"

They turned into the driveway, which now was lined with yellow. Bea was all smiles as she came out of the front door to meet them. Nothing pleased her more than to have someone else enjoy her flowers. She was like a parent showing off her child. The flowers were her babies now that everyone in the family was gone.

Marvin was certainly impressed, and when he got a whiff of what Marcia had told him, he said, "Ha! You were right, Marcia. There's a real nice spice scent here!" Marvin was appreciative of nature in general. Of course, nothing would ever mean as much as the apple trees and the scent of the blossom, but he enjoyed it all.

Bea told him she was going to give them some iris roots in the fall, and he let her know that he was happy about that. He leaned over again and took another whiff, declaring his appreciation. Bea had her scissors ready and cut off several of the ones that still had the second bloom to come. Someone once said Irises have a special quality of serving the second helping. When the first flower was finished, the second one replaced it.

Bea said, "Come on in, and I'll wrap these stems in wet paper towels for you. If you aren't going right back home, I'll put 'em in a vase of water. You won't want to leave 'em in a warm car for very long. They're pretty delicate, you know."

They were just going down to the country store and would be going promptly back home, so the watered-down paper towels would be just fine.

"Thank you so much, Bea. I'm going to put them on the kitchen table so we can take a whiff every time we pass by," said Marcia. *What a pleasure that would be!*

Bea asked Marvin if he heard all about the trip to see Rachael. He said he had and couldn't wait to see the pictures. "Me either. I'm tellin' you, it was a wonderful day. We all enjoyed it. I just can't thank you enough, Marcia, and I'm gonna send a note to Barbara. She's a sweetie."

Bea went back into the house. She was glad that they had stopped by. She hadn't seen anyone for a couple of days.

She sat down in her usual chair in the living room and turned on the television. It kept her company most evenings although she didn't pay a lot of attention to it. She used to have a little dog that was good company, but he died, and she didn't have the heart to lose another one. She had been through too much "losing."

It's hard to be alone. I'm not cut out for it. This television is just a bunch of noise as far as I'm concerned. What's on today? Anything worth watching? She turned the dial through the news (all bad), zipped past those raunchy sitcoms, and found a rerun of *Lawrence Welk*.

This is better than some of that stuff people seem to like these days. I wish there was a baseball game. She always loved baseball.

She had cut the grass earlier, washed up, eaten a bite, and now felt quite tired. She liked working outside in the yard, but it was getting harder and harder all the time. She would not give in. If she had to, she'd take two days to cut the grass, or three, but she was not going to have someone else do it. Everybody else seemed satisfied to let Silas cut their grass. Not her. *Maybe they all have more money than I do, but I need every cent of my Social Security to get by. I have to do what I have to do.*

She had always done whatever she had to do. Her husband "Brick" had been gone for twelve years, and her children had moved away. Her son wanted her to move in with him, but she'd rather stay in her home with her memories. She and Brick built this house with their own hands—a pretty fine house too. She didn't know much of anything about construction. Brick knew a little, and together, they found out how to do a lot more and did it. As a bricklayer, he had seen many homes constructed, had asked a lot of questions, and decided he could build his own. He was right, largely because he had a wife willing to be his helper.

"Those were the days" as they say. They really were.

Bea and Brick—the team. Everyone thought of them that way. They were a team, all right. They even won dancing contests together.

She sat back in her chair, closed her eyes, and thought of those wonderful moments.

When she opened her eyes, reality appeared, and she recognized the awful truth.

I won't be dancing anymore.

ϒϒϒ

Across the street, Adele was dozing in her chair. She had seen Marcia and Marvin stop at Bea's house, and she smiled when Marvin bent over and smelled the irises. As she watched, she drew in her breath, imagining that lovely fragrance. Marvin sure seemed to appreciate the scent. He would. He was a really sensitive kind of person.

She looked lovingly toward Marcia, recalling how much she enjoyed the trip that Marcia had planned for all of them on Wednesday. It was a wonderful day with her friends and Rachael, and lunch was delicious at the restaurant. She hoped they didn't talk too much and too loudly for the rest of the patrons, but they were enjoying themselves so much that perhaps they did get carried away somewhat. Well, no one complained, and they had one of the best days in a long time. She was glad she had Bea for a friend. Bea was so fun-loving and almost childlike in her appreciation of the simple joys of life. They had been friends even before their husbands died. They all four loved to play euchre, and would squeeze time when they were younger to play cards together. *We sure don't have to squeeze time in these days. Time is what we have the most of with little to do to fill it. Isn't that ironic? I do still have my daughter to see often, which is more than most of the others have. I should* go visit her tomorrow. Will she know me this time?

Her daughter Candice and her grandson Billie had lived with her for many years after the horrible accident. Billie grew up and took over the care of his mother. His wife Samantha was a gem to have married into the situation as it was. She had said she loved Billie and Candice too. She felt it was the right thing to do and has never complained about it as far as Adele knew. Billie always said that Samantha and Candice were the best of friends. His dear wife was truly one of God's best. Adele knew that she would not be able to care for Candice now and was thankful for the way it all worked out. Adele's other daughter, Mildred, offered many times to relieve Samantha for a week or more. She would possibly have the opportunity over the summer while Billie and Samantha take a vacation. That would be good.

She was thinking about how her daughters enjoyed one another when they were younger. When they would sing duets in church, everyone said their voices blended perfectly. She looked at the picture of Candice taken when she portrayed Laurey Williams in the high school musical *Oklahoma*. She had just recently taken the picture out of storage. It had always been too heartbreaking to see. It was still difficult, but somehow comforting too.

Candice had great promise. I'll always remember her that way.

I'll go call Samantha and let her know I'm coming tomorrow. Maybe she'd like to go out for a couple of hours, and I'll sing some songs to Candy that she knew.

Adele later looked out of her window and was wondering if there might be something she could do that would be more productive. The sun was setting behind a hill. It was such a beautiful sight that she continued to stand there until the sun completely disappeared. The clouds developed into beautiful swirls of orange and purple, and the sun's rays projected from behind the hill with beams of light reaching to the heavens as the last breath of the day's undertaking. It was beautiful, and she felt that God was giving her a promise of brighter days and more hope for her future. She felt peaceful and relaxed and knew that whatever the Lord had planned for her would be for His glory and her joy.

"*I lift up my eyes to the hills* . . ." she quoted and realized that, as she looked to the hill, she was raising her concerns to the Lord who would send His help to her. She slept better that night than she had in a long time.

32

A "Getaway"

The choir at West Hope Church had the month of June off because Francine would not be there to direct them. There was a young man from a neighboring community, who played piano pretty well, and he agreed to play for the church services; however, he had no training in choral directing. Most of the choir members had sung in the choir forever, and at West Hope, the choir did not usually take any time off—by choice. In fact, they didn't feel comfortable sitting in the congregation.

Francine and Lawrence were as excited as children as they packed to go to Florida. They would spend the entire month there, coming back after the Fourth of July holiday. The session of the church insisted. After all, Francine was a child of the church and had been ever so faithful. She certainly deserved the month off, and more if she would take it. They would manage.

"I won't be long, Lawrence. I simply want to be sure that Mother has everything she needs. I'm not worried about her. I know that Darrell will look after her very well while we're gone, and Paula is going to be calling her daily. Did you fill up the car with gasoline?"

"Yes, it's ready to go. When you get back, we'll just put these suitcases and supplies in and we'll be ready too. I'll fill up the thermos with coffee and the water jug with ice."

"That's just fine. I'll be back real soon."

Francine had a lovely last-minute visit with her mother, returned home, and she and Lawrence gathered up the final items and were off. What a great day it was! Francine felt as free as a bird. Her mother was very happy that she was getting away, and she wouldn't let her linger to do anything more than was absolutely necessary, which was very little.

Francine and Lawrence planned to take a leisurely trip through the West Virginia mountains by way of Interstate 79 and Route 19, as the scenery through that ruggedly beautiful state was as picturesque as any in the country.

They gravitated toward I-79 and were well on their way south, devoid of responsibilities for a while. Lawrence had retired, but as with most retirees, he found quite a lot to keep himself busy—mostly with Habitat for Humanity, utilizing the skills he'd developed through a hobby of woodworking over the years. Francine was now retired as a schoolteacher, but she considered her work at the church her real occupation—the one that had always been first on her priority list, and she was devoted to it. She would never retire from doing what she believed she was assigned to do by a Higher Authority, and until she had a better signal that she should vacate being the principal musician at the church, she was not going to; however, she certainly did believe that retirement was possible—perhaps probable—and felt led to pray about it.

Now here they were, finally, on their long-awaited vacation. They passed Morgantown, West Virginia, and the view increased in beauty the farther along they traveled. Connecting to Route 19, the hills reached even higher to the sky. They were so densely covered with trees that they blended into a splash of green. One tree was indistinguishable from the rest. The road turned this way and that, but it was so well engineered that they had no difficulty navigating it. Every turn in the road presented a new scene, and they were in constant awe of this untouched beauty.

They stopped at Tamarack, the fantastically beautiful and unique cooperative outlet for West Virginia artisans. It was both fine and troublesome that they had chosen to make this stop because it was so amazing and enjoyable that they stayed longer than they had anticipated.

Leaving all of life's pressures behind, they decided to linger a little longer to have dinner. They had a bed-and-breakfast reservation in the mountains farther south, and it would be held for them no matter when they arrived. They could just phone ahead, which they decided to do.

They both opted for the rainbow trout, which would be pan-fried right before their eyes. Mmm, mmm. Lawrence knew immediately what to add to his dinner plate: kale greens cooked with bacon and onions! This was a true West Virginia Appalachian meal, typical of the other artisan labors of the establishment.

"I have never eaten kale before. I'm not sure I would like that," said Francine.

"Well, you can taste mine if you want. Do you like cooked spinach or any other kind of greens?"

"Believe it or not, I love dandelion greens. We have always gone out all over the farmland at home and gathered dandelion greens early in the spring before the flower formed. That's when they were the tenderest. My mother would wash them over and over to get the mud off from the spring rains, and she cooked the greens with bacon or ham. Oh my! How we looked forward to that!"

"Well, sweetheart, I think you should try the greens here then. You sound like a cultured gourmet in quality eating!"

They laughed. She ordered the cooked kale as he did and watched the cooking of the trout. They picked up some good breads and fruits, gathered up their food (which was cooked and served cafeteria-style), and found a very nice table away from the whereabouts of people.

The meal was "lip-smackin" good, they said as they made an effort to assume the position of good ol' West Virginia hillbillies. They declared that they were off to a very good start on their journey.

They had seen some beautiful handmade quilts there and decided that they would certainly be in good competition with a couple of the ladies back home—some compliment. The woodworking demonstrations and items for sale just amazed Lawrence. He could never have made anything so beautiful, he told Francine. She didn't question that because she honestly had never seen such fine polished furniture.

They bought a mouth-blown bowl that they both liked very much and a beautiful embroidered dresser scarf for Lawrence's mother. She would love them.

What a beginning to a delightful trip! If this were any indication of how much they were going to enjoy themselves, they would be thrilled all the way. Well, it was, and they arrived in Florida as two relaxed, joyful people in very good spirits.

It was going to be a wonderful vacation for everyone. Lawrence was especially pleased to find his mother feeling much better these days, which made everything just perfect.

33

She's Floored

The choir at Center Church in Innesport was not taking vacation time during June—or July either. Their normal vacation was in August; however, Janine would not be scheduling practices because they could sing familiar anthems during the summertime. It's a good thing that she did not have to run into the city to work on new music or practice the choirs because she could not possibly have done so with all the things that were on her plate.

The house in Innesport hadn't sold, so they didn't have to pack up everything there immediately. They turned to preparing the new house for their move, which included deciding upon paint colors and other issues. They were seriously thinking about remodeling the kitchen but wondered whether it would be better to do that now or later.

"I think we should move in and use the downstairs kitchen while we go ahead and do the remodeling upstairs once and for all. Then we won't be tearing up everything later," said John.

"I can live with that. Who do we call to have it done, or were you thinking of tackling it yourself?"

"I know my limitations, hon, and designing and installing a kitchen is beyond my expertise. You would be the better one to design it, and then we'll get a contractor to do the job. However, I think we could put new flooring down ourselves. I've been looking at the new laminate, and the instructions look fairly easy to follow."

"Okay, let's check into it."

They went to one of the big hardware stores and found the kitchen that they thought would look great in the new house. They contracted them to come, measure, and work with Janine on the final design. The kitchen expert walked with them over to the flooring section to assist in selecting coordinating flooring, which they penciled for ordering when they had the correct measurements.

The contractor met them at the new house the next day. He and Janine worked with several designs before a decision could be reached.

This took more time than either expected because Janine had been working in the same kitchen for twenty years. Consequently, she didn't have an up-to-date knowledge of the conveniences that modern technology could provide. The contractor actually had to convince her that she would appreciate and be able to use these new technical advancements.

"John, would you come here, please?"

"What's up?"

"I know you wanted me to decide upon everything in the kitchen, honey, but I need your opinion about some of these new appliances and such."

He jumped at the new ideas with time- and work-saving benefits. "No sense in buying a horse when you can have a car."

There he goes again!

"Actually, they no longer make some of the things I thought I should have," she said. "I guess I've been living in another era and didn't even know it."

"Times, they are a-changin', they say, so I guess we might as well face up to it."

He convinced her, and they signed the papers for the new cabinets, appliances, and installation.

In a few days, the old kitchen was completely gutted so that John and Janine could *easily* install the flooring. John spent an entire day preparing the base for the flooring, confidently setting up *horses* to use for sawing purposes, checking his rotary blades, etc. After that, off they went to pick up the laminate and supplies required.

"This will be fun, Janine—working together on a major project. Wait 'til the kids see what we've done."

That attitude changed quickly. What began as *fun* turned into *tedious* and *exhausting* and could have ended even the best of relationships!

"Let's see. It says here—"

Yes, it looked easy on paper, but for two people past middle age to be getting up and down, up and down, reading instructions, cutting boards . . . then down again, and up again. It was one of the most backbreaking jobs they could have done. The children would have helped, but "oh no!" They could handle it themselves!

"John, I think we went beyond our limitations, after all. I can't move! My knees hurt, my back hurts, and my shoulders hurt. I probably won't be able to play the organ on Sunday. You have reached your limit too. I can tell. Admit it."

"Okay. I admit that it's not been as easy as I originally thought, but we can finish this, Janine. One more day, and it will be done. Then we can stand back and be really proud of ourselves while the contractor does the rest in here. Can you handle just one more day, or do you want me to call Greg to come over?"

"No! Please. I don't want to have to do that! Do you see where we have come? It is one of the deadly sins—pride! Now I know why it is called deadly! This pride *will* kill us."

"You know that pride doesn't kill you! Pride puts you on your own instead of trusting and depending upon God for help. We begin to think we can do it all. That's what pride is all about. It's a turning from God. It really has nothing to do with us doing this floor without God helping us."

"John, I'm getting irritated with your biblical interpretation . . . but I still have a comment, if you don't mind."

"Go ahead."

"I'm tired. I hurt, and I have not thought of God for the past few days. Here we are grumpy with one another, trying to do something we are not good at, determined to make an impression to others—showing off that we actually did it ourselves. I don't think we are where we want to be. I don't like it."

"I'm sorry, Janine. You're right.

"Look at us," he continued. "We are making this move in answer to God's call, and what are we doing? We're attacking one another, trying to do too much around here instead of fixing *ourselves* up for what lies ahead. We need to slow down and stop driving ourselves like this. It's my fault! I had no idea this flooring thing would be so tough on us."

"John, we have one more day to finish this. I'm sure we can. But please, please, let's not get ourselves into this kind of situation again. Okay? Next time, let's get help or absolutely not worry about it."

They finished it, vowing to behave differently in the future. Janine was always the one to strive for perfection, so John had figured she would have to have everything perfect before moving into the house. She knew that, realizing that she had to change her view of herself.

"This is harder than I thought it would be," Janine said. "Are we really going to be able to do this?"

"I'm not going to get us into any more projects, I promise."

"No, no! I mean making all of these changes in our lifestyle and living up to our commitment."

"Of course! Maybe God is testing our faith and our trust in Him. Even though you were directed to follow this path, it doesn't mean that everything will fall right into place. Let's trust that God is still with us and strive to move ahead with confidence and faith."

At this moment, she was reminded why she fell in love with this man. He was "Mr. Solid-as-a-Rock!" He would be right there with her all the way . . . *and maybe he will rub my back.*

ϓϓϓ

"Hello! Is anyone home?"

John recognized Kathy's voice. He was in the master bedroom putting a fresh coat of paint on the walls. "Come on in. I'm here in the back."

"Hi. How's it coming?"

"Good. Good. Your mother just left. She had to go find some boxes. Do you have any?"

"I don't know. I'll have to look, but Greg can get you some over at the dairy—some good strong ones. You can borrow them."

"That sounds good. I'll tell your mother. How's this look?"

"Beautiful. You are a terrific painter, Dad."

"Well, thanks, but if you think that compliment will get me to paint all of your rooms, think again!" he said laughingly.

"Did you see the kitchen?"

"What about it?" "Oh, never mind."

"What . . . I'm going to go look."

He smiled as he imagined the reaction.

She called from the empty kitchen with the beautiful laminate flooring. "Wow! You really mean business, don't you? What's the deal? You're getting a completely new kitchen, I see."

"Well, didn't you?" he asked as he came in behind her.

She smiled. "We did. Who's doing the work? The floor is fabulous!"

"I'll have to get your mother to tell you. You know how I am with names." He didn't want to tell her without Janine being there. They should have called the family over when they had finished, but they just didn't take the time.

"Well, I thought I'd stop by to see if you need any help. I'm sorry that I didn't stop sooner, but with the end of the year at school and reports to be filed, I haven't had much time. I finished up today, so call on me anytime. Okay?"

"Okay, honey. Thanks. I'll tell your mother to give you a call later today."

When Janine came home, John told her of the visit by Kathy. They had a good laugh over it. Janine called Kathy and said that the family should all stop over that evening.

When the four of them arrived, they all went into the upstairs kitchen. When everyone had finished with their "oooo's and "aahhh's" about the flooring, they let it be known that they had done all of it themselves.

"Why didn't you call?" asked Greg.

"Well, at first we decided we wanted to 'do it ourselves.' Then when we got fully into the project, we began to realize that maybe we *couldn't* do it at our age, and *shouldn't* do it, but were too darned stubborn to admit it to anyone. By then, we were just determined to see the foolish decision through to the end." John was giving it to them straight. It felt better than just standing back and letting them think they were two people who could do just about anything.

"Well, it's beautiful . . . It really is. But please don't do any more," Kathy said.

"Ha! Don't worry about that!" Janine was firm in her response.

"Don't tell us you are going to install the cabinets." Greg was not sure about these two.

Janine quickly responded, "No! Not a chance. We're finished with such foolishness. We're having a skilled and qualified contractor do that. The cupboards are cherry. We had almost chosen the oak because it had more of a rustic look, but the house isn't really built that way, and cherry seems to be more fitting."

Janine went on to tell them about the new appliances. Greg got a good chuckle out of that. He knew all about modern technology in the kitchen.

"You'll enjoy them after a while. It won't take long," Greg said.

"Practice makes perfect!" quoted John. Janine knew that was certainly true.

They went downstairs and had coffee, sodas, and snacks. The girls loved the big family room. They talked about Claire coming soon. *My goodness! It's almost July!* Janine thought.

Where does the time go?

They all left the house around the same time. John and Janine went on into town, and Kathy and her family headed on down the lane. Someday that would change.

34

Holding On

The following week, when she was finally able to move about without feeling like a ninety-five-year-old woman, Janine began clearing out the house in the city.

First, she drove over to the church, hoping to find Pastor Jim, and she did.

"Well, Janine, how are you getting along in your move?"

"Slowly, actually, but I think we'll be ready to move officially in a couple of weeks."

"Is something on your mind?"

"Yes, I guess there is." She sat down at his invitation. "I still have no idea where I'm going with this endeavor, Jim. When I look ahead, all I see is something like a shield or a fog. Nothing is clear to me."

"Are you feeling uncomfortable as though you've made a mistake?"

"No . . . not at all. I'm feeling *impatient* more than anything, I would say. I'm positive I have been led. No doubt about it. I could never look back at the encounter with the Holy Spirit and dismiss that as something not true. It was real. It still is, but nothing more has come to me in any way at all. Like I said, it's as though I'm walking into the future in a haze or something."

"You *are* being impatient. I've heard of situations like yours, Janine. Sometimes it takes a while before we can be sure of what to do next. Keep praying."

"Well, that's another thing. I seem to be at a distance from the Lord right now. I don't feel His presence as I did before. Sometimes I ask if He is really there, and sometimes I don't get an answer either. I'm a little nervous about myself. I'm not unsure of God's purpose. He has one, that's for certain. I'm unsure of my ability to comprehend—to be open to what He wants of me."

"It's a difficult time for you. You have too many things crowding in. When you get things settled and you can back off from doing so much, you'll need to take the time to focus on the Lord. The Bible tells us to 'be still.' Remember the little wind?"

She nodded. She was definitely still in a rush and a whirl.

"Be still, Janine, and wait for the Lord to speak to you.

Will you work toward that?"

"I will! It's what I want more than anything!"

"Can I make one suggestion?"

"Of course! Please!"

"I'm feeling that you should let go of your work here at Center Church. I can hardly say this, Janine, because it means so much to us to have you here, and I know you love your music.

But I am almost certain that you need to separate yourself from us and begin anew."

"Oh my! That scares me. It really does. I haven't actually considered it seriously."

"Let's pray about it."

As they prayed, she recognized that she had returned to her old ways of depending solely upon her own capabilities. She felt the tension inside of her. She felt her arms folded tightly, her teeth clenched, her eyes pressed shut, and she knew that she was behaving like the little wind.

"Jim, you are so right. I realize that I'm trying to do more than I should. I am not putting everything in the Lord's hands because that is against all that I've ever required of myself. I will consider what you've said about resigning from my position here at Center Church. Perhaps I should. There was a time when I believed that I was being 'called' and was totally in accord. What has happened to me? I'm still holding on, Jim. I haven't let go at all!"

"Don't be so hard on yourself, Janine. There is a lot of physical activity involved in moving. It's draining you and taking a lot of your energy. You are making headway, and don't for a minute believe that God has forgotten about His Plans for you as He is affectionately working behind the scenes making everything ready. Consider this your time of preparation too, Janine. Remember Ecclesiastes? 'There is a time for everything.' I don't think the word 'preparation' is specifically mentioned, but the 'everything' covers it well. You cannot move ahead until the preparations are complete—yours and His."

She went over to her house on Alamont Street, and instead of packing boxes, she put on her walking shoes.

Her walks had been so valuable, and she had not taken time to do that lately. She could hardly wait. It was so hot outside today; maybe she'd have a stroke walking in the heat. *No. I will not. It is God's will. I will walk and talk and be with the Lord as He is calling me to do.*

"Christ be with me." She felt His presence, and her spirit lifted to be with Him. She was buoyant and was not weakening with the heat. All was well, and she felt encouraged to make a decision.

She came back to Alamont Street and saw that John had come home also. Perfect! She wanted to talk with him.

"Hey, where have you been? I called you on your cell phone, and it rang in your purse here. Where did you go without your purse? I was a little concerned about you."

"I'm fine, really. I needed to go for a walk."

She needn't say more—John knew.

"I'm going to submit my resignation to Center Church. I went to see Pastor Jim this morning, and he told me he felt that I would be doing that, anyway. We prayed about it, and then I went for my walk and talked it over with the Lord. It's clear that this is what I need to do."

"Fine. I have no problem with that, Janine. Maybe I should resign from the session also. What do you think?"

"John, I can't tell you to do that. It must be your decision."

"Well, we'll see. Now, tell me . . . how are you going to stop the music? It is so much a part of who you are."

"The way I see it, God is not going to give me something new to do if I am clinging to doing what I've always done."

"Right."

She appreciated his gesture of understanding.

Janine had a pleasant and meaningful conversation with Charlotte, the choir director, concerning the developing situation. With confidence in Charlotte's willingness to continue on her own, Janine typed the letter of resignation and addressed it to the clerk of session. She telephoned Pastor Jim to let him know it was being put in the mail with a copy being sent to him also.

"The session is going to be set back over this, Janine. I don't know what you have written, but if John is at the meeting, he'll most likely be asked some questions of concern."

"He'll be there. He knows of my decision and supports me in it."

"I'm happy for you, Janine. Don't worry about us. We are a big church. There will be musicians eager to work with us. Will we ever find such dedication as we have had over the past many years? We'll certainly be praying about it, and we'll be praying for you too as you go on your way."

"Thank you so much. May God bless us both, Jim, and all those in partnership in the Gospel."

She took her letter to the post office, dropped it inside, and walked out with trust and confidence.

"John . . . one thing. If there is mention of a send-off, please let them know that I do not want that. It would be very hard for me. I prefer to write a letter in the next newsletter, as I mentioned in the resignation. Please reinforce that for me, will you?"

"Yes, I will. So, you will be participating in Worship the first Sunday in July. Then you will be finished. Right?"

"Right."

"It's inevitable, Janine, so no sense in delaying. 'Lost time is never found again.'"

ᵛᵛᵛ

The newsletter was out, and so was the information concerning Janine's resignation. The telephone would not stop ringing. John had to pick up the calls to keep Janine from losing her mind. She had calls from the women, neighbors, her past students, and people in the community who had worked with her over the years. It was nice to know that they cared about her; however, she just didn't want to talk about it so much, having said everything she could in the church newsletter about answering a *call* from the Lord. Of course, she realized everyone's dilemma with that. She previously didn't understand that expression, either. A call from God is not, as a rule, understood by many.

When she went to church the next Sunday, she could not get away from the crowd that gathered around her. She wanted to tell everyone of her love for the Lord and her desire to serve Him, but it was impossible with all the questions that were coming her way. The questions pelted her from several directions at once.

The only way she could handle that, in all honesty, was to meet one-on-one with her friends, which she hoped in time she would do. She could also speak at a meeting for those who would like to hear her story, she supposed. That might be fair, after all—and wouldn't God want her to witness for Him? Well, she'd just wait for all that as time passed. Right now, she still had to finish up at the church by organizing the files, and she would do so promptly.

She finally had everything boxed up at the old house and could turn it all over to the mover. *Hallelujah!* She hoped and prayed she would never, ever have to move again.

There was a cleansing aspect to it, though. Why, oh why, was she holding on to so many old things? She called the Salvation Army who gratefully arrived one morning with a truck to accept all and anything she would give away.

The truck drove away, weighed down with a lifetime of accumulation. *No. No. I can't just let it all go. I should have stopped them. That was the sofa we had when we first got married, and I kept it for all these years. The chandelier with several missing parts hung in our first apartment, and we retrieved it when they tore down the building for safety's sake.*

I loved that old chandelier. John said the baby bed was totally unsafe. I think we could rebuild it . . . but for whose baby?

Oh, Janine. Let it go! Let it all go! You must! she said to herself.

"Janine . . . Janine? It's okay," John said. "This is the perfect time to get rid of things we should not have kept in the first place. 'Holding *on* is holding *back.*'"

"I never heard that one before. Who said it? It's pretty good."

"John Stephens."

"So now you are a philosopher, along with all of your many attributes. I'm constantly amazed at this man I married."

She gave him a big hug. He returned it generously, and that was just what she needed. His confidence, assurance, and love strengthened her, and she wanted to always be holding on to John Stephens . . . even to the end of her days.

The End

Q and A for the Author

Do you know your characters as well as it seems?

I have been given the opportunity to know many persons of the older generation over a lifetime. I believe that God has caused me to be drawn to those who were older than myself so that I would understand their needs, their strengths, their beauty. And yes, those characters you have read about do exist—not necessarily as individuals, but as blended personalities from people I have known and loved over the years.

Why do you not describe the physical characteristics of your ladies?

I want my readers to see them as they will. One could freely be the reader's mother, friend, or sister. If that person in the book is described as "tall, thin, and somewhat bent over with arthritis," the opportunity to find the person in the reader's own family may be lost. This is a book about heart and about personalities. It has little to do with outward appearances. I hope that each reader can feel what my characters feel, place themselves in the person, or place a loved one there. I do not want outward appearances to override that, and I must say that I have heard from a number of people that characters in this story are also found in their churches or family. "I know ladies just like these," are typical responses.

Why did you write this book?

First of all, God gave it to me to write. I give him the glory for any good it accomplishes. We want to reach out to the elderly, but more than that, we all need to know these beautiful persons as real people with feelings of pain, love, humanity, humor, vibrancy, and helpfulness. We should not push them aside as used up with nothing to offer. They are wise and full of experience, and they love to interact with us and with others. We would be wise to encourage such activity.

This story continues in the second book of this trilogy, "Blessed Abundantly" as Janine and the Ladies of West Hope are brought together to find more blessings than any of them would have thought possible. As each day develops spirits are lifted and joy abounds as the ladies enter into a new phase of life that changes everything.

Personal contact: *wordsnmusicmjb@gmail.com*
Website: *www.maryjeanbonar.com*

About the Author

Mary Jean Bonar has always been immersed in the field of music. She taught piano lessons for many years, directed church choirs, and had the amazing opportunity to train and direct (in Minneapolis) an International vocal choir of perhaps ninety members. Her expertise in handbell ringing was in demand and this led her to train others within her tri-state area; and of course she was the Handbell Director for her church.

She has demonstrated her love and interest in her community by freely serving on the Board of Directors for the United Way, the Local Cemetery, and the Washington, PA Symphony Orchestra.

Mary Jean is the mother of four, grandmother of seven, and great grandmother of five. "The Beat Goes On" could be said as members of the family, near and far, continue participating in church music to this day.

Mary Jean responded to words spoken by the Holy Spirit to begin writing her book. Having such a close relationship with the Lord, she recognized His call, and the story that is in your hand represents the beginning of an exciting experience for her. She says that the characters became her best friends, and the time spent with them will be cherished forever.

Looking back, Mary Jean remembers she always enjoyed writing. Lately she wrote a "personal blog" nearly every day of the Christian Lenten Season to her family and friends, and when Lent came around again she sent forth a study of some of the most beloved Psalms of the Bible.

More author information can be found at
www.maryjeanbonar.com

Characters of note in *Look to the Hills*

Those related to or in the lives of Janine and John Stephens

Janine—church musician, middle aged, and volunteer community leader, reliable perfectionist

John—husband, church leader, easy-going, great father

Kathy Lang—older daughter of J & J, lives in log home with two daughters, husband and dog, faithful to God

Greg Lang—husband, dairy chemist, the "Chef" **Karen**—teenage daughter of Kathy and Greg **Meghan**—younger daughter of same **Prince**—a very loving and smart Black Lab

Deborah Franklin—younger daughter of J&J, lives in Pittsburgh, teaches French, enjoys social whirl

Dr. Robert Franklin—husband, no children, strongly dependable

Harry Stephens—son of J&J, lives in Oklahoma, hard-working, loves the land and his family, easy-going like his father

Rhonda Stephens—wife, helpful to her husband and sons <u>William</u>, <u>Charles</u>, <u>James</u>—growing up in open spaces

Claire—French exchange student

Center Church in Innesport

Rev. James Faulkner (Pastor Jim)
Connie—secretary.

Others

Gloria—proprietor of Gift Shop
Cindy—piano student and bride

Those in or near West Hope, Pennsylvania

West Hope Church

Rev. Daniel Campbell (Pastor Dan)
Wife Pat—both loved by all.

Iola MacCowan—hard of hearing widow, teacher, still has a lot to offer but few will listen to her; enjoys meetings at her house

Anne Kendrick, has husband, **Owen,** large house. She is sensible, intelligent, still drives, belongs to organizations

Rachael Wimbler, widow, huge smile, creative with her hands, cooks for her son, has overcome adversities

Adele Marsh, widow, has disabled daughter, grateful for her many blessings, prayerful

Julia Gillanders—quiet, unassuming widow, lives on Main St., former first grade teacher. Her own children have moved away

Jenny McMurray—good friend of Julia's but has moved out of West Hope and only occasionally can attend church

Beatrice Roberts—"Bea" widow. loves baseball, dancing, good times; works hard to keep her spirits high as she grows old

Laura Davidson—husband, **Edward,** is not well. Married over sixty years, lives on farm with cattle. Children are near enough to help.

Marcia and Marvin Severight—own the Apple Orchard and Orchard Restaurant. She is loving, caring and a help to many

Harriet Burnett—Sunday School teacher. Younger than all the ladies, but is a widow, belongs to several service organizations

Francine Cook—marries **Lawrence Simmons**. She is the organist at West Hope Church.

Alice Cook—Francine's mother, oldest church member; can recite many biblical passages and usually wins Bible Trivia games

Paula and Kevin Kirkland—own a beautiful farm near the West Hope Church. Paula is a quilter. Kevin a strong church leader, raises cattle

Hayden and Elda Carter—own the General Store in West Hope, ready to lend an ear or a hand

www.ingramcontent.com/pod-product-compliance
Lightning Source LLC
LaVergne TN
LVHW091539060526
838200LV00036B/666